LOCAL VOICES/
GLOBAL PERSPECTIVES

LOCAL VOICES/
GLOBAL PERSPECTIVES

Challenges Ahead for U.S. International Media

Edited by Alan L. Heil Jr.

To order copies of this book, contact the Public Diplomacy Council:

Public Diplomacy Council
School of Media and Public Affairs
The George Washington University
805 21st Street, NW, Suite 410
Washington, DC 20052 USA
Telephone: 202-994-0389
Email: pdi410@gwu.edu
Web site: www.publicdiplomacycouncil.org

ISBN 978-0-9764391-3-4

The findings, interpretations, and conclusions expressed here are those of the authors and do not necessarily reflect the views of the Public Diplomacy Council or any organization affiliated with the authors.

Contents

PUBLIC DIPLOMACY COUNCIL

The Public Diplomacy Council (PDC) is a nonprofit organization committed to the academic study, professional practice, and responsible advocacy of public diplomacy.

PDC members believe that understanding and influencing foreign publics, and dialogue between Americans and the citizens of other countries, are vital to the national interest and the conduct of 21st century diplomacy.

The Public Diplomacy Council was founded in 1988 as the Public Diplomacy Foundation. Dedicated to fostering greater public recognition of public diplomacy in the conduct of foreign affairs, the Foundation evolved to serve also as a resource and advocate for the teaching, training, and development of public diplomacy as an academic discipline.

In 2001, the Foundation joined with The George Washington University School of Media and Public Affairs and Elliott School of International Affairs to establish the Public Diplomacy Institute.

The Foundation changed its name to the Public Diplomacy Council in 2002 and became a membership organization with an elected board of directors. The Council maintains close ties with the USIA Alumni Association, whose president is an ex officio member of the Council's board of directors.

The Public Diplomacy Council has no government connection and receives no financial support from any government source. It seeks support from foundation grants and corporate gifts.

The Council is a 501(c)(3) organization that relies on the dues, contributions, and volunteer work of its members. Donations to the Council are tax deductible.

INTRODUCTION

Alan L. Heil Jr.

"Words are sacred. They deserve respect. If you get the right ones, in the
right order, you can nudge the world."

—Tom Stoppard[1]

"The ancestor of every action is a thought."

—Ralph Waldo Emerson

FOR MORE THAN SIX AND A HALF DECADES, American publicly funded
overseas broadcasters have offered a wealth of words, thoughts, and ideas
to hundreds of millions of curious citizens. In the twentieth century, these
beacons of hope served national security in both World War II and the
Cold War mainly through radio broadcasts via shortwave and medium wave
or FM relays. Their commitment to accuracy and reliability as sources of
news, information, and inspiration made the radios a daily window on the
day's events in nearly every region of the world.

Yet, in the view of a prominent group of American business
executives:

> Our political parties, members of Congress, and presidential candidates
> need to take a serious look at why America is losing its friends around
> the world and urgently assess what can be done to reverse this alarming
> trend. It is no exaggeration to say that the United States is now facing a
> reputation crisis of global proportions—and this crisis must be addressed
> by creative thinking and vigorous new initiatives in public diplomacy.[2]

Among the activities most in need of wholesale reform is U.S.
international broadcasting. Our government overseas broadcasts today

---

Alan L. Heil Jr. was deputy director of Voice of America, 1996-98, and acting director,
November 1996 to April 1997. He is author of *Voice of America: A History* (Columbia
University Press, 2003).

operate in a global environment that bears scant resemblance to that of even twenty years ago. Then, a former BBC World Service executive took a prescient look at a new communications age when he said, "It's no longer 'I fired a signal into the air; it fell to earth I know not where.'"[3] Today, digital satellite communications and the rise of the Internet have changed all that in a single generation. Today, it is no longer one-way communication. It is an increasingly interconnected, online, "real time" media world that is linked in nanoseconds. In this wireless, multimedia planet, millions are both content receivers and content producers. There is an exciting, increasingly uncharted dialogue in global discourse. It is, specialists say, a new and infinitely challenging viral media environment. In the words of one analyst: "The rapid expansion of the Internet and broad availability of digital media have resulted in unprecedented communications that will favor the agile agent in our global village."[4]

This book is a compendium of views by a wide range of scholars and practitioners of international broadcasting past and present, both in the United States and abroad. It is designed to serve as a guide for confronting the challenges ahead for U.S. government–funded international broadcasting in a new era. There is bipartisan agreement that America's taxpayer-supported civilian voices overseas are in dire need of reorganization and greater investment. They must, after all, be "agile agents," flexible enough to identify and react to the constantly shifting new ways people seek and share information, yet wise enough to capitalize on long-established core assets. The questions are: What is the programming mission, and how do we best achieve it, technically? How do we structure our overseas broadcasting arms, and most important, to what end? How do the growing numbers of public service nongovernmental producers of audio, video, and text fit in?

All of these networks collectively reach a global audience easily exceeding 150 million radio listeners, television viewers, and Internet readers each week. They remain indispensable to the nation's security and global stability. For that reason, the Public Diplomacy Council hopes that policymakers in the new national administration and new Congress of 2009 will find in these pages a compelling justification for a broad, in-depth, independent, professional review of the overseas networks' goals, organizational structure, and resources needed for success in a rapidly changing communications world.

A rich variety of notions about the future of U.S. international broadcasting is outlined here. The architects of a new way ahead will face many choices as they determine the future of America's government-funded overseas networks. The options that emerge must demonstrate a potential to (1) match audience and national needs, (2) determine resources needed to perform the mission, (3) factor in the role of the private sector and business community in the nation's media outreach, and (4) explore ways of retooling an unwieldy superstructure that, if anything, has added many more redundant layers since the Cold War.

How America's Overseas Networks are Organized

The anatomy of U.S. international broadcasting is bewilderingly complex. Today, there are five principal U.S. taxpayer-funded overseas networks, relatively little known in America but widely recognized abroad:

- two federal civil service government broadcasters, the global Voice of America, and Radio and TV Marti to Cuba in Spanish.
- three grantee broadcast networks, which are privately incorporated but government funded: Radio Free Europe/Radio Liberty (RFE/RL), Radio Free Asia (RFA), and the Middle East Broadcasting Networks Inc., consisting of Radio Sawa and Alhurra Television in Arabic.

All five networks are guided by the principles outlined in the International Broadcasting Act of 1994 (Public Law 103-236, see appendix 1) and the Foreign Affairs Reform and Restructuring Act of 1998 (Public Law 105-277). The latter act consolidated the U.S. Information Agency into the Department of State. Many have come to consider that legislation a mistake, especially since 9/11. The nation would be better served, some specialists believe, by a separate independent government or private nonprofit agency or agencies coordinating all the elements of national outreach—policy advocacy, educational and cultural exchanges, and broadcasting—to reflect American ideas credibly and foster a free flow of information in an increasingly hostile and anti-American world.

Under the 1998 act, those five international broadcasting networks are administered by an autonomous Broadcasting Board of Governors (BBG, see figure 1). When the new U.S. administration takes office in 2009, the Board will have been a separate overseer of these entities for almost a decade. A management consulting firm concluded in 2006 that there is no professional broadcasting structure in either the private or public sector resembling the BBG.[5] This part-time board of presidential appointees—four Democrats and four Republicans plus the Secretary of State—has, for many of the past six years, supervised the networks as a day-to-day manager would. In nearly all other networks surveyed by the firm, on the other hand, boards of directors perform broad oversight and overall financial control. They entrust management and daily operations to a full-time network CEO or CEOs reporting to those boards.

FIGURE 1. BROADCASTING BOARD OF GOVERNORS

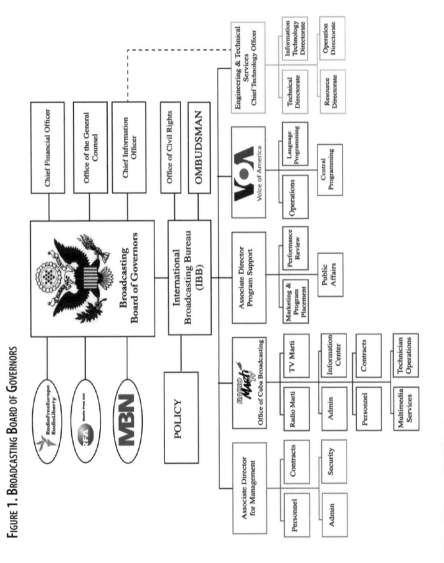

The BBG supervises two types of networks. One is exemplified by VOA, chartered by Congress to provide accurate, objective, and comprehensive news and information about America and the world as well as a balanced projection of American thought and institutions (see appendix 2). In addition, VOA must explain American policies and national debate on these policies to audiences everywhere. The other principal U.S. international broadcasters are the so-called surrogates, such as RFE/RL, RFA, and the Martis (see appendices 3-6).[6] These, too, are wholly funded by the U.S. Congress, but they are designed to serve as alternative media to individual regions where authoritarian governments restrict the free flow of information within their own borders or crack down on internal dissent and a free press. In general, VOA is regarded as official, long-term, and strategic. RFE/RL and RFA, as privately incorporated nongovernmental entities, are taxpayer funded and generally considered tactical. Engineering and technical services are provided to all the networks by an overarching support directorate known as the International Broadcasting Bureau (IBB).

AN OVERVIEW OF THIS SURVEY

This book had its origins in a forum on U.S. international broadcasting co-sponsored by the Public Diplomacy Council and the George Washington University School of Media and Public Affairs held on November 16, 2006. A grant by the Stuart Family Foundation of Chicago made publication possible. The Council wishes to thank the Foundation and former USIA Director Bruce Gelb for their support and endorsement of the project. Several of the essays that follow are transcripts or updated versions of presentations made originally at the forum. Other analyses introduce entirely new insights and appear here for the first time. Text editor Kris Rusch merits special thanks for her skillful blending of these analyses.

The anthology is designed to enhance understanding of the problems and prospects of U.S. international broadcasting in six parts. The first part, "Setting the Scene," comprises a pair of essays. One is by former Public Diplomacy Council President McKinney Russell, based on his brief history of U.S. international broadcasting at the 2006 forum, and the other, by the current Council President, Robert T. Coonrod, is a follow-up analysis of the many choices that lie ahead for policymakers and the private sector.

Part 2 poses the question: "Who's listening and who might do so in the future?" Contributors to the discussion of research challenges, impact, and approaches to international broadcasting, past and present, are Morand Fachot, a Switzerland-based international media consultant; Graham Mytton, the former head of research at the BBC World Service who counsels broadcasters on site all over the world; and Paul P. Blackburn, a former USIA senior Foreign Service officer who followed international broadcasting closely during his tours in Asia.

Part 3 is a collection of essays and case studies looking at future U.S. international media programming options. Sanford J. Ungar, president of Goucher College and former director of VOA, calls for a renaissance of that U.S. flagship global network. Myrna Whitworth, former VOA acting director and director of programs, updates her presentation at the November forum to define the eclectic new programming requirements inherent in today's rapidly evolving interactive media environment. Jeffrey Trimble, program director of the Broadcasting Board of Governors and former acting president at RFE/RL, offers a reprise of his forum address on why surrogate broadcast programming worked in the twentieth century and continues to be effective. In a concluding discussion of programming to the Middle East, we present two contrasting views. One is by Salameh Nematt, an award-winning journalist of *Al Hayat* newspaper who has reported for many years from and about the Arab world and who spoke at the forum. The other is an original contribution by Brian T. Conniff, president of the Middle East Broadcast Networks Inc. that oversees the around-the-clock Arabic language U.S. networks, Alhurra Television and Radio Sawa.

Part 4 begins with Council member John H. Trattner's comprehensive prescriptions for the future structure and resource requirements of U.S. overseas broadcasting, based on his experience as a prominent American public affairs consultant and former Department of State spokesman. This is followed by the forum remarks of Mark Helmke, senior staff aide to the Senate Foreign Relations Committee ranking member, Senator Richard Lugar of Indiana. This part ends with a roundtable discussion of structure and resources by two retired U.S. public affairs officers, Walter R. Roberts and Barry Zorthian, who served at VOA during its very early years and offer veterans' perspectives on the way ahead.

In part 5, we explore the many ways new media can be deployed in the interactive, interconnected world of user-generated content. Dr. Nicholas J. Cull of the University of Southern California's Center on Public Diplomacy, another Council member, begins by explaining how new and old media can be blended in a comprehensive strategy for twenty-first century global broadcasters. Engineer Mark Maybury of the Mitre Corporation then discusses how new media tools can enhance public diplomacy efforts. Adam Clayton Powell III, USC's Vice Provost for Global Affairs, updates his forum talk with descriptions of latest developments in the world of iPods, reality TV, Second Life, myCNN, and other recent entrants in the brave new world of multimedia. Finally, Gary E. Knell, CEO of Sesame Workshop, describes the impact abroad of *Sesame Street* and its success in gaining hundreds of millions of viewers in Egypt, India and other countries.

The final part, "A Vision for the Future," features four seasoned executives and specialists in U.S. international and public broadcasting. James K. Glassman, chairman of the BBG, leads off with a focus on the mission and purpose of U.S. international broadcasting, drawing from his years of experience as an editor, author, and nationally syndicated columnist on financial matters. Kevin Klose, president and board member of National Public Radio and former president of RFE/RL, follows up by citing objective journalism and credibility as attributes of overseas broadcasting aimed at promoting civil society and individual liberties in countries reached. The anthology concludes with a roundtable on the future of international broadcasting by the IBB's Dr. Kim Andrew Elliott, an internationally known specialist in the field speaking as a private citizen, and Ambassador William A. Rugh, a Council board member and author of *Arab Mass Media* and editor of *Engaging the Arab and Islamic Worlds through Public Diplomacy*.[7]

A Foundation For Looking Ahead

"Why did the West win the Cold War?" asks author Michael Nelson, former managing director of Reuters News Agency. "Not by the use of arms. Weapons did not breach the Iron Curtain. The Western invasion was by radio, which was mightier than the sword."[8]

Flash ahead to Burma as we see it today and Associated Press dispatches of late September and early October, 2007:

> Lines formed at stores in Yangon (also known as Rangoon) for shortwave radios, with people eager to tune into BBC, Radio Free Asia and Voice of America … Others also count on the Internet, which was shut down after protesters effectively used it for weeks to publicize the growing protest and subsequent crackdown … A pro-government newspaper, the *New Light of Myanmar*, accused the BBC and VOA of dishing out "a skyful of lies" and called the two news organizations "saboteurs."[9]

A review of the essays in this book underscores three conclusions about the nature of U.S. international broadcasting today:

1. Its credibility—its core ethical principle—remains basically intact. Burma is only one of many recent examples of the respect this engenders in countries where the media are dysfunctional or regime controlled. There are scores of additional examples, such as RFA's in-depth reports on a coal mine explosion in Heilongjiang covered up by PRC media, and RFE/RL's courageous reportage on its Radio Free Iraq service that cost the lives of two of its contract field reporters there.

2. Its content—accurate, objective, and balanced journalism—reflects attributes resembling those normally associated with the most effective public diplomacy. At one time or another, to paraphrase from Nicholas Cull's essay, international broadcasters:

- **listen** using interactive programs, call-ins, chatlines, and audience research focus groups;
- **advocate**, reflecting American policy and policy debates;
- **teach** through English language instruction, historical analyses, and reporting best practices in democratic governance, rule of law, combating poverty both in the United States and overseas; and
- **foster** people-to-people relationships, through programming about U.S. exchanges and through international media training (more than 7,000 journalists from at least 140 other countries over the years).[10]

In addition, according to contributors Cull, Morand Fachot, and Myrna Whitworth, an established network brand name is essential. In this regard, writes Cull, VOA, RFE/RL, and the BBC "are the Evian and Perrier" of broadcasters.

3. It retains its capacity to be a voice for the voiceless in nearly every region of the world. Whitworth, Gary Knell, and Mark Maybury make this point in illustrating how programming of the future might continue to center on (1) alleviating quality of life issues such as lack of education, unemployment, discrimination and injustice that breed terrorism and ethnic strife; and (2) the importance of children and women in radio, television, and peer-to-peer Web site exchanges of the future.

"New audiences," writes veteran Radio Canada International Program Manager Elzbieta Olechowska,

> are not helpless captives starved for information. They look around, pick and choose and jump at the opportunity to share with others what they think, see, know, and dream of. The times when the station knew better than their audiences what it was they wanted and what turned them on are past and will not return. While there is still a place for solid journalism and excellence in broadcasting, the advent of interactivity means that the age of radio has evolved into the age of the audience.[11]

For policymakers shaping the future of U.S. international broadcasting, the horizons are vast. In the twentieth century, over-the-air media such as radio and television dominated the electronic marketplace of ideas. Today, there is in addition a whole new cyberspace arena in which to share these ideas.

Hope rather than fear should prevail in the ideas marketplace.

Many more millions participate in a complex web of one-to-one or one-to-many communications relationships. The ultimate challenge will be to combine these delivery systems intelligently. Programs that concentrate on alleviating poverty, ignorance, disease, and environmental degradation are most likely to serve both America's needs and those of its many audiences. Hope rather than fear should prevail in the ideas marketplace. Credibility will remain a force multiplier of soft power. Managed adroitly, new and traditional media will help produce what clearly is in the nation's long-range interest: a more stable, more democratic, more peaceful planet.

Notes

1. Newsletter to the staff of the Associated Press by former AP Managing Editor Mort Rosenblum, January 31, 2006.
2. Tom Miller, "America's Role in the World: A Business Perspective on Public Diplomacy" (New York: Business for Diplomatic Action, 2007).
3. BBC World Service Managing Director to the VOA staff, 1989.
4. See Mark Maybury, chapter 15 of this book.
5. Booz Allen Hamilton, report to the BBG, July 22, 2006.
6. Although it is a federal agency, the Office of Cuba Broadcasting (Radio and TV Marti) assumes the role of a surrogate station. It is located in Miami, Florida.
7. William A. Rugh, *Arab Mass Media: Newspapers, Radio, and Television in Arab Politics* (Westport: Praeger Publisher) 2004; and *Engaging the Arab and Islamic Worlds through Public Diplomacy* (Washington, DC: Public Diplomacy Counci, 2004).
8. Michael Nelson, *War of the Black Heavens: The Battles of Western Broadcasting in the Cold War*, (Syracuse University Press, 1997), xiii.
9. Associated Press dispatches, September-October 2007.
10. See Nicholas J. Cull, chapter 14.
11. Elzbieta Olechowska, *The Age of International Radio: Radio Canada International (1945-2007)* (New York: Mosaic Press, 2007), 267.

PART 1
SETTING THE SCENE

1. A Voice for Change

McKinney Russell

THE STARTING POINT was seventy-nine days after Pearl Harbor. It was in February 1942 that the United States rushed to get into the world of international shortwave, where it had never been before. On the first day, it sounded like this: "Hier spricht eine Stimme aus Amerika" (This is a voice from America speaking). The announcer went on to make this promise: "The news may be good for us, or bad. We will tell you the truth." This has been the goal of U.S. broadcasters ever since.

Soon after World War II, the Cold War provided its own quite urgent drive to get on the air—this time to the closed communist-controlled societies—and by 1951, the Voice of America (VOA) was broadcasting in forty-five languages. Today the VOA claims a worldwide weekly audience of more than 115 million, which includes a television audience of 42 million.

Back in the 1950s, the intensifying Cold War spawned America's so-called surrogate broadcasters, chiefly Radio Free Europe (RFE) and Radio Liberty (RL). Radio Free Europe broadcast to Eastern Europe and Radio Liberty to the Soviet Union. For several decades, the two Munich-based stations had covert funding from the CIA. The VOA, located in Washington as part of the U.S. Information Agency, continued "telling America's story to the world" and covering global as well as U.S. news.

Meanwhile, RFE/RL's thousand or so broadcasters framed their news and messages through the national perspectives of their listeners, meaning that both stations' broadcasters spoke as free and democratic Kazakhs or Romanians or Uzbeks. An essential part of their mission was letting their audiences know what was happening in other parts of the communist world by cross-reporting, for example, about effective agricultural reforms in Poland that may work in Russia or Ukraine.

There was back in the 1950s an initial troubled period of hard-hitting rhetoric, when words like "rollback" and "liberation" were in vogue. When

McKinney Russell is former president of the Public Diplomacy Council (2001-2007) and a retired career minister in the U.S. Foreign Service.

I began work as a correspondent in Munich in 1955, Radio Liberty was still called Radio Liberation, and it didn't become Radio Liberty until 1959. In time, RFE/RL, like VOA, worked hard and with a great deal of success to live up to high journalistic standards. There were a few lapses like the misleading signals given by some RFE broadcasters during the Hungarian uprising in 1956. But as revered VOA director Henry Loomis liked to say, the surrogates and VOA are like two blades of a pair of scissors. They needed each other to cut well.

By the early 1970s, the Congress and the Nixon administration had decided that covert CIA funding of RFE/RL was an anachronism—everybody knew about it anyway—and Congress made some significant changes. The Board for International Broadcasting was established as a bipartisan entity that took appropriations from the Congress and channeled them to the broadcasters, that is to say, to RFE/RL. Voice of America continued on its own track. The Board was charged with oversight of their operations to make sure—and this is rather interesting cautious language of the time—that their programs were "not inconsistent with the broad outlines of U.S. foreign policy."

They stayed that way. They exposed the cruelties and inequities of the system, and the communist structure collapsed. No one can measure with certainty the role of U.S. broadcasting in bringing down the Berlin wall and communism, but I think no one doubts that VOA, RFE, and RL, with their devoted audiences of many millions, were a powerful force for resistance and for change. Among those who have said so are Lech Walesa, Vaclav Havel, Alexander Solzhenitsyn, and many others.

Radio Free Europe and Radio Liberty left Munich and moved to Prague at the invitation of the Czech government in 1995. In many cases, the Radios got permission to use local transmitters in countries that had formerly been hostile. Radio Free Europe/Radio Liberty broadcasts in Polish, Hungarian, and the Baltic services were abolished as free media took root in Eastern Europe. Then, with urging from the Congress, RFE/RL began broadcasting to non-European audiences. Broadcasts to Iran and Iraq began as early as 1998. In 2002, broadcasts in Afghanistan's two principal languages were restored after a brief initial run in the early 1990s. Today, there are twenty-eight languages broadcast from Prague under the RFE/RL banner. Nineteen of those twenty-eight are to predominantly Muslim nations.

As far as VOA is concerned, it continues its journalistic mission with a good deal of energy. Although twenty of the languages of the VOA have either been reduced or eliminated over the last several years, VOA has moved very actively into television and Web-based news. Twenty-five of VOA's language services on radio now also have television services, as well.

The VOA's parent agency, USIA, was folded into the Department of State in 1999. Then the VOA and all of the other networks were placed under the purview of the Broadcasting Board of Governors (BBG), along with RFE/RL, Radio Free Asia (RFA), Radio and TV Marti, and the Middle East Broadcasting Networks, which include Radio Sawa and Alhurra television in Arabic.

It is a very complicated chorus of voices to manage. A quick glance at the organizational chart of the BBG will reveal the complex network that the BBG oversees. It has nine members, four from each of the two major parties, and the Secretary of State is designated as the ninth member of the BBG. Her designee on the BBG was, until recently, Karen Hughes, the former undersecretary of state for public diplomacy and public affairs. As boards go, they're quite active. They meet once a month and, with the help of a professional staff, exercise oversight of the stations' programs to ensure their quality. At the same time, the BBG functions as a firewall to protect the Radios from outside political pressures that might damage their credibility.

> No one can measure with certainty the role of U.S. broadcasting in bringing down the Berlin wall and communism, but I think no one doubts that VOA, RFE/RL, with their devoted audiences of many millions, were a powerful force for resistance and for change.

In 2006 and 2007, the BBG proposed cuts in English and a score of other languages at VOA, RFE/RL, and RFA. There were some rather sharp objections by a number of people on the Hill and elsewhere. Both the Senate and the House of Representatives reversed the proposed cuts in English late in 2007. Now Congress has before it a new budget, and it is considering the latest BBG programming priorities in U.S. overseas broadcasts throughout 2008.

A BBG decision to close down VOA Arabic altogether in 2002 was followed by the creation of Radio Sawa for Arab listeners in the Middle East. It has aimed at building a new youth audience, via FM relays and a lot of popular music. Another network, Ahurra television, was launched in 2004. Both have provoked questions about the value of attracting large audiences over attracting perhaps a fewer number of listeners who want serious, substantive programming. Radio Farda, broadcast in Persian to Iran, follows a similar format of entertainment plus some news.

Important questions remain. First of all, how should U.S. broadcasters choose their audiences to strengthen the impact of broadcasting, and are our audiences large enough, diverse enough, and potentially influential enough to justify the continuation of these stations in their present form?

Second, what kind of programming and media are most effective in today's rapidly changing media landscape?

Third, is there a way to streamline the current, complex structure of international broadcasting? Can it be improved in any way?

Finally, there is a question of resources. The current level of funding for international broadcasting is over $600 million a year, nearly half the entire public diplomacy budget of the United States. The questions are: is that level adequate, is it sustainable, and is it being allocated and spent as well as it should be?

In the pages that follow, contributors to this volume will share their sharply divergent views on these and other broadcasting themes.

2. New Media and the Future of Broadcasting

Robert T. Coonrod

U.S. INTERNATIONAL BROADCASTING gets attention and increased funding in times of conflict. It is an effective instrument of war. Its origins, its glory, and its recent revival can only be understood in the context our response to national security threats. When we feel safe, we neglect it. That is also the case with the other pole of our nation's public diplomacy—cultural diplomacy. Both international broadcasting and cultural diplomacy are getting renewed attention and funding today, as we face a murky, non-state adversary. We have trouble defining who or what it is. We deploy all of our defenses. Ours is a rational, if myopic, response. And it underscores the timeliness of this volume.

If we can understand why U.S. international broadcasting has been successful in the past, if we can gain a better appreciation of its scope and capacity, and if we can draw a clearer picture of the challenges we face, perhaps we can imagine and promote policies that are both rational and farsighted.

Why has our international broadcasting succeeded? There are probably as many glosses on that question as there are people offering opinions, but the fact of its success is important. As we look to the future, can we learn from our success and adapt accordingly? Or will our past success be an impediment, tempting us to pursue an outmoded way of thinking and acting?

My own view is that in our rational myopia, we seldom looked beyond the fact of the success of U.S. international broadcasting to ask *why* it succeeded. How were we able to speak to disenfranchised people around the world—in their own languages as well as in English—that promoted them to respond as they did? There is abundant anecdotal evidence that it was the nature of our engagement with them, not the forcefulness of the

---

Robert T. Coonrod was president and CEO of Corporation for Public Broadcasting 1997-2005, and was the CPB's executive vice president and CEO from December 1992. He currently serves a president of the Public Diplomacy Council.

message, that mattered most. We could be trusted. We were reliable and relevant. And when conditions permitted, we also listened.

We should also look for parallels between U.S. international broadcasting's success and the successful twentieth century global penetration of U.S. commercial media that did not rely on national security threats to advance. America's cultural dominance was fed by commerce, creativity, and innovation.

The challenge to the people who manage and plan the future of U.S. international broadcasting is very real. William Gibson had it right: "The future has already arrived. It's just not evenly distributed yet."

A case in point: the Broadcasting Board of Governors (BBG) takes understandable pride in the development and effectiveness of its satellite-delivered TV broadcasts—this at a time when focus globally is shifting toward Internet Protocol Television and the build out of high-speed, flexible G3 networks.

Commercial media have an advantage because they choose their markets. The BBG entities, in contrast, respond to priorities; they are challenged to be present in almost all markets and on all media. What's the best way to do that? How can the United States have a multimedia dialogue with the world in the century before us? As a January 2008 report of the Defense Science Board Task Force on Strategic Communication makes clear, it will be difficult.[1]

The explosion of new communications media and the attendant social change will make it ever more difficult to frame constructive communications based on a genuine, positive correlation of interests. In the short term, it will be literally true that the more we know, the less we understand. A "gotcha" or "zero-sum" attitude will likely predominate. This will benefit our adversaries.

As traditional barriers to the flow of information collapse, the speed with which information will circulate and the ubiquity of information sources will overwhelm people's ability to distinguish important from trivial. Image will overwhelm context. For U.S. government–supported media, the seeming contrast between our principles and our actions will be even more apparent.

The growing generation gap will add additional complexity. In most developing societies, the percentage of youths in the population is rising rapidly, as that percentage decreases in most developed countries. Nearly half the world's population now lives in cities and is under twenty-five years of age. Young people's access to new and more information sources will amplify distrust of traditional sources that often emanate from what they view alien cultures and societies.

The report goes on to point out that the viral nature of electronic media, coupled with the growing proliferation of electronic communication devises, means that almost every action or operation that can be witnessed can also be recorded, distributed, manipulated, and distorted. Individual actions will be amplified. The good news is that censorship will become a practical impossibility. The bad news is that even small, tactical military actions will be viewed globally and may achieve strategic significance.

> The viral nature of electronic media, coupled with the growing proliferation of electronic communication devises, means that almost every action or operation that can be witnessed can also be recorded, distributed, manipulated, and distorted.

Then there are the domestic challenges.

In 1942, no one disputed our nation was at war. There was widespread mobilization and overwhelming support for the war effort. It is different today.

The U.S. Census Population Clock has now passed 303 million. The population has more than doubled since Voice of America's first broadcast. Our common language and homogenized national culture sometimes obscure our growing ethnic, racial, and religious diversity. The United States of America is rapidly becoming one of the most ethnically and culturally diverse nations in the world.

None of this is inherently good or bad. But in an era of globalized, viral media it adds another thick layer of complexity. The growing many-to-many communication model will accelerate the spread of unmediated information. Rapid Internet growth in developing countries will amplify it as it transforms markets, media, civil society, and even a variety of conflicts in a less stable world. The shift in our own society away from balanced, validated reporting to polarized, opinion mongering will also be amplified as it circulates abroad.

Even the opportunities will be challenging. The NGO phenomenon offers unprecedented opportunities, if the BBG or its successor organs can figure a way to work with it. America's long experience with community radio and its recent toe-in-the-water testing of low-power FM offer the opportunity to use low-tech, low-cost, traditional media to bridge communication divides. Can its proponents and the U.S. government make common cause? Producers of independent media are now also linked electronically. Traditional gatekeepers are easily bypassed.

At the other pole is Hollywood. Many decry its homogenizing effect on our global culture; yet, many executives in Hollywood—all of whom stand to make a lot of money if they are right—argue that the forces of globalization are actually promoting cultural diversity. Hollywood, in the words of Sony Pictures CEO Michael Lynton, "is becoming as diverse as it is universal."

These are not, to quote Walt Kelly's Pogo, "insurmountable opportunities," but they do require a thoughtful, sustained, disciplined, strategy, not in response to a perceived threat, but in the service of an affirmative interest. We cannot do any of this without a reasoned debate. Let's start it now. There are many opinions to be heard and many interests to be considered. This volume, we hope, offers some of the best of both.

Notes

1.   Defense Science Board Task Force on Strategic Communication, available online at www.publicdiplomacy.org/37.htm/.

3. Reaching Audiences to Survive and Prosper

Morand Fachot

INTERNATIONAL BROADCASTING is very specific and complex: to reach diverse foreign audiences it must meet a large number of very different audience expectations while helping to fulfill certain foreign policy goals of the governments who fund these broadcasts. International broadcasting has gone through a number of different phases from its beginnings in the early 1920s, corresponding to major historical events (World War II, the Cold War and its aftermath, and 9/11) that have influenced its development.

JOURNALISTIC VS. POLITICAL PRIORITIES

The success of Western broadcasting to the Soviet bloc during the Cold War can certainly be attributed in great part to the precedence given to journalistic priorities over political considerations. However, in the post-9/11 period, the priorities of U.S. international broadcasting seem increasingly dictated by political factors and as such cannot hope to achieve the same results as during the Cold War. Nowadays, the emphasis is on projecting a positive image of the United States, regardless of audiences' needs and expectations.

The priority traditionally given to the key performance indicators focused on news (a trustworthy source, unbiased and objective, and relevant) has given way to precedence for statistics measuring a favorable impression of the United States.

For people used to decades of official propaganda, such as those in the Middle East, this concern with image seriously undermines the credibility of U.S. broadcasts, which are more and more perceived as veering toward propaganda. This is corroborated by the relatively low level of trust accorded to stations such as Radio Sawa or Alhurra TV in the Arab world. No new service or greater output will alter what is essentially a widespread perception in these countries that U.S. policy is fundamentally one-sided and anti-Arab/Muslim.

Morand Fachot is a media analyst and international broadcasting consultant.

BUILDING AND RETAINING LOYALTY

For international broadcasters, compelling content, consistency, and respect for listeners are essential to build trust and audience loyalty, and to survive or even thrive in what is now a very competitive and fast-changing global electronic media landscape. Limited resources mean that broadcasters need to evolve while maintaining their identity.

> For people used to decades of official propaganda, such as those in the Middle East, the concern with image seriously undermines the credibility of U.S. broadcasts, which are more and more perceived as veering toward propaganda.

International broadcasters' content is very different from that of domestic operators: it must be tailored to the needs of the target audiences, but not limited to them. A genuine international outlook is necessary and should differentiate international from domestic broadcasters. Another important aspect of international broadcasting is special programming that meets specific needs, such as encouraging vaccination campaigns, promoting land mine awareness or health issues, and encouraging post-conflict reconciliation. Offering that compelling and unique content is the key to the success of an international broadcaster.

Broadcasters, international and domestic, should engage more with their audiences, sharing ideas rather than "shouting" them. Obviously, not every program can evolve to the same extent, but international media analyst Jonathan Marks argues that simply pushing lists of statistics and commentaries across a border is not effective, either.[1]

International broadcasters have been around for a long time; the BBC, Deutsche Welle, VOA, Radio Free Europe, and Radio Liberty are all recognized brands, an asset that should not be neglected. However, to the foreign observer, U.S. international broadcasting seems to be declining: well-established services are being cut or scrapped altogether instead of being revitalized, and new services are being launched under a different name or brand. This duplicates effort, wastes resources, and confuses audiences. As International Broadcasting Bureau analyst Kim Andrew Elliott once put it there are "too many Voices of America."[2] Operating under a single brand, the BBC World Service doesn't suffer from this. It is probably the best-known broadcasting brand in the world, enabling it to be instantly recognized and to attract new audiences as it launches new services, such as an Arabic or Farsi TV, or enters new markets like it did in the United States.

A strong brand and consistency are essential in developing a loyal audience. The experience of French international broadcasting is a sober reminder of that. Over decades it has changed names, scrapped services without prior warning before re-launching them years—sometimes even months—later. It is undergoing constant changes even today. With the exception of Francophone Africa and the Middle East, where its Arabic-language station Monte Carlo Doualiya (formerly RMC Middle East), a well-established brand had—in its last available survey (2005)—over 10 million listeners, the audience for French external radio in other markets is mostly insignificant.[3]

CHANGING GLOBAL MEDIA LANDSCAPE

One of the most serious challenges facing international broadcasters is the fast-evolving and increasingly competitive global media landscape. U.S. and other Western international broadcasters enjoyed a near monopoly in the offer of alternative programming some twenty years ago, in particular to the Soviet bloc, the Arab World, and Asia. But today they confront a plethora of competitors, thanks to the end of state monopolies and the opening up of markets to commercial operators, new delivery modes, and the emergence of new media. Another major uncertainty concerns the future media consumption patterns of the younger generation.

Eastern Europe and some countries of the former USSR were quick to adopt the Western model of broadcasting with a mix of commercial and public broadcasters offering a diversity of programming and better news coverage. Changes in the Middle East can be traced back to the first Gulf War. Arab viewers turned to CNN, which, at the time, was the only satellite provider of television news to the region. This quickly led to the launch of a number of pan-Arab satellite services, the best known of which is Al Jazeera. As of August 2007, there were some 370 free-to-air satellite TV channels broadcasting to Arab viewers. Asia experienced the same expansion, albeit later.

Given the preference of audiences everywhere for television over radio—and in the case of radio for the superior audio quality of FM over medium wave (AM) or shortwave—it is obvious that traditional international broadcasting (built mainly around shortwave and AM broadcasts) must evolve to survive. However, an over-reliance on gatekeepers, controlling distribution, and new technology (local FM and AM relays, satellite broadcasts, Internet services) is hazardous. There are countless and recent examples of governments rescinding re-broadcasting licenses, banning FM relays of international stations, and controlling or cutting Internet access (Russia, Côte d'Ivoire, China). Therefore, keeping shortwave and AM is not an outdated and costly option, but essential, as recent events in Burma show: Western international broadcasters, the BBC, VOA, and Radio Free Asia, as well as the Oslo-based domestic surrogate broadcaster Democratic Voice of Burma, all available on shortwave, were the only non-official sources of news for the Burmese. According to a 2005 BBC World Service Trust survey, more than two-thirds of radio listeners in Burma listened to the BBC and 38 percent to VOA at least once a week, certainly a lot more during the recent crisis.

International broadcasters can offer an alternative source of news, not just in countries where information is restricted, but also in countries where it isn't. This is the case in the Indian-controlled part of Kashmir, where media equipment and daily use of electronic media, as well as audiences for international broadcasting stations (from the United Kingdom, United States, and Pakistan), are higher than in other parts of India.

CASE STUDY: INDIA

A look at how a major player, the BBC, is faring in India can offer interesting insights into how an international broadcaster operates in a large and disparate market undergoing sweeping changes, which audiences it has, and how it might best meet future challenges to remain relevant.

In 2006, the BBC World Service had an estimated audience of 19.2 million to its six language radio services broadcasting (on shortwave and AM alone) to the region, making it the leading international broadcaster in the country. Most of its audience (around 83 percent) is concentrated in five states; overall radio listening in the country (traditionally one of the lowest in the world) has been severely eroded by growing TV access. The BBC World Service audience is highest in the states with the lowest TV penetration. Private FM stations are boosting radio listening in the main cities, but are not allowed to broadcast news (although this may change soon).

What distinguishes the BBC is the high markings its listeners give it in three key performance indicators (a trusted source, unbiased and objective news, and relevant news), where it scores higher than all its competitors, domestic broadcasters included (between 86 percent and 62 percent for the three categories in the five states). Other indicators show that nearly 90 percent of listeners say they expect to continue listening to the station in five years and that they would continue listening even when they have access to TV. These are clear signs of listener loyalty.

In terms of audience, the following tentative conclusions can be drawn from this market. First, the vast majority of listeners are not opinion-formers who can access a number of outlets including, but not exclusively, international broadcasters. Rather, the majority of listeners are the less affluent part of the population. This is a trend observed elsewhere, particularly in regions where information is tightly controlled or in crisis hotspots. Second, in spite of these positive results in India, the BBC, like other international broadcasters, needs to face up to a fast-changing environment and the challenges it will pose in the future.

The recent and dramatic expansion of BBC TV and radio services in India shows that the broadcaster is aware of this and adapting its offer to the changing market conditions.

RAPIDLY EXPANDING MARKET

The Indian broadcast media market is under-equipped, but it is the world's fastest growing (18.5 percent a year, compared with China's 16.8 percent). This exceptional growth, which is a useful indicator of what is happening (or will happen) in other countries, raises a number of issues regarding the future of international broadcasting in the region and elsewhere.

First, most radio listening is still done through shortwave or AM; only 263 FM stations (161 of state-controlled All-India Radio and 102 private) were operating in India in August 2007, with 175 more FM stations to go on air by the end of 2007. The compound annual growth rate (CAGR) of the radio sector to 2010 is expected to be 32 percent.[4] FM radio is boosting overall radio listening but eroding audiences to shortwave and AM, the main channels for international broadcasting. To retain their audience, international broadcasters must secure FM re-broadcasting agreements when and if the ban on news on FM stations is lifted.

Second, only about half of households (100 million) have a television, 40 percent of which are black-and-white sets. About 60 percent of TV households have access to cable or satellite. About a hundred new TV channels will be launched in the next twelve months, and 700 are expected by 2009. The satellite operator Tata Sky forecasts 165 million pay-TV households by 2015. The sector's projected CAGR to 2010 stands at 24 percent.[5]

Third, television access is eroding radio listening; the audience for international TV news channels (BBC and CNN) is relatively small and mainly to be found in urban areas, reflecting the general limited grasp of English. The growing number of vernacular and English news channels also means more competition for these two channels. However, the launch of international TV news channels in other national languages by international broadcasters to gain a larger audience, if worthwhile, would be costly.

Fourth, the prospects for cable TV distribution of radio programs are not promising, as almost no one ever uses it to access radio.

Fifth, there are some 180 million mobile phones in India today, and 500 million are expected to be in use by the end of 2010. Internet use is still relatively low but expanding rapidly. Internet Protocol TV and broadcasting to mobiles are being rolled out. For international broadcasters, this may present attractive alternative channels for the distribution of audio, video, and text content.

RECOMMENDATIONS

A number of recommendations can be drawn from this market (and others, particularly in the Arab/Muslim world) for U.S. international broadcasting:

1. Journalistic considerations should always prevail over political priorities to ensure audience trust and loyalty. Government input should be limited—in consultation with broadcasters—to the definition of target areas and languages, and possibly to the volume of broadcasts.
2. Rely on and maintain or increase funding for established brands; there is no need for new ones.
3. New ways to deliver content must be constantly explored to retain and gain listeners and viewers, as the changing media landscape is eroding international broadcasters' audiences; a multimedia, multi-platform approach is essential.
4. Targeting opinion-formers is important, but it should not be the overriding priority. Reaching the largest possible audience most in need of diversity of news is the priority. Quality and diverse content are key to reaching both audiences.

Notes

1. Author interview with Jonathan Marks, October 21, 2007.
2. Kim Andrew Elliott, "Too Many Voices of America," *Foreign Policy 77*, Winter 1989-1990, 113-131.
3. With Radio France Internationale's decision to close down its local relays in Moscow, Saint Petersburg, Vilnius, Sarajevo, and New York, and plans to close its FM relays in Cambodia and Laos, the broadcaster may become irrelevant in many markets.
4. Federation of Indian Chambers of Commerce and Industry – PricewaterhouseCoopers 2005 report on Indian Entertainment and Media Industry.
5. *Ibid.*

4. PROGRAMMING AND DELIVERY FOR INTERNATIONAL BROADCASTING

Graham Mytton

RADIO REMAINS THE ONLY MEDIUM today that is accessible to nearly the entire population of the world. It remains the most widespread medium of communications and the only medium that is impossible or extremely difficult to block access to. For many people in the world, especially those most marginalized and vulnerable, radio is the only medium they can access with any reliability.

My remarks are based on research conducted by InterMedia for the BBC World Service and for various U.S. government–funded broadcasters, such as Voice of America (VOA), Radio Free Europe (RFE), Radio Liberty (RL), Radio Free Asia (RFA), Alhurra, Radio Sawa, and the others. Some recent data raise questions about the wisdom of some actions of the major international radio broadcasters. First, I want to look at the global situation with regard to radio, shortwave in particular, and then I want to consider the particular facts about shortwave and the way in which people access the various technologies available to them.

In the world today there are just over 1 billion households with a radio set. That means that most people in the world have access to a radio set. Access is lowest in China, India, Bangladesh, Pakistan, and some other Asian countries. It is highest in several European, African, and American countries.

What about the actual use of radio? In a few countries, radio has become a very weak medium. In China, for example, radio listening has fallen to a very low level. More than twice as many Chinese now have a cell phone as have a wireless radio set. India is another country in which radio is weaker than one might expect, largely as the result of the growth of competitive satellite TV entertainment and news services. But elsewhere, generally speaking, radio is in good health and not in decline. Indeed, in many areas, even in well-developed markets, radio is showing signs of real growth.

Graham Mytton was head of audience research and the first controller of marketing at the BBC World Service.

What about *shortwave* radio? The highest level of access to shortwave is found in some of the poorest and most unstable countries in the world: Afghanistan, Iran, Burma, East Timor, Uganda, Sudan, and several other Asian, African, and Middle Eastern countries. The lowest level of access to shortwave is in North America, parts of Europe, and some other Asian countries (see figure 1).

But access is not enough. What really matters is the extent to which people actually use shortwave to listen to radio. Here again we find that the highest level of shortwave use is in countries that have the greatest need for information and where the media are under some degree of state interference or control (see figure 2).

The data show that radio in general and shortwave in particular remain powerful media in certain areas, but weak in others. The highest levels of shortwave use, according to the latest surveys that I have seen, are to be found in some Gulf countries, Afghanistan, Burma, Nepal, Sri Lanka, Kenya, Nigeria, Rwanda, Zambia, and several other sub-Saharan African countries. There has been decline in some countries, but if we look at global data for the major international broadcasters, shortwave services remain the primary way in which listeners access international broadcasting. In 2006,

Figure 1. Shortwave Households (percentage)

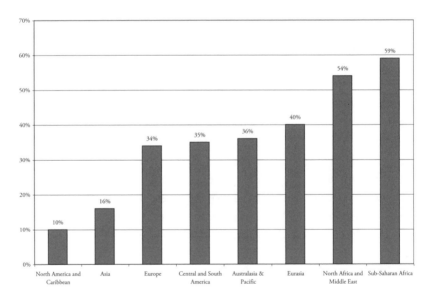

Note: Eurasia refers to most of the former Soviet Union, excluding only the Baltic States, plus Afghanistan, Iran, and Turkey. Asia refers to the rest of Asia but excludes the Arab countries.

FIGURE 2. WEEKLY LISTENING TO SHORTWAVE (PERCENTAGE)

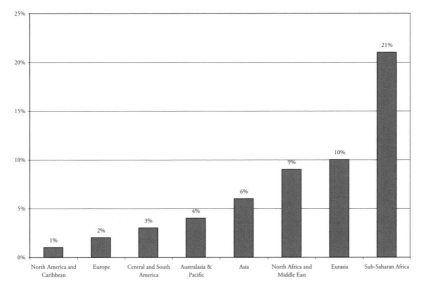

Note: Eurasia refers to most of the former Soviet Union, excluding only the Baltic States, plus Afghanistan, Iran, and Turkey. Asia refers to the rest of Asia but excludes the Arab countries.

the BBC World Service announced a new global audience calculation of 183 million weekly listeners to its various radio services. The BBC, rather sheepishly it seemed to me, admitted that most of these listeners still access the BBC using shortwave. The BBC, like many other major international broadcasters, has made some major cutbacks in shortwave in recent years. It is now difficult in some parts of the world to hear the BBC World Service at all, except via occasional rebroadcasters. Despite this, the audience has grown, and what's more, there are more listeners on shortwave than ever before. Indeed, the proportion of shortwave users among the global audience may well be higher than the official figures, as current audience measurement projects tend to focus on urban areas and areas where the BBC has FM relays and rebroadcasting arrangements. However, areas where shortwave remains strongest tend to be under-surveyed or even ignored altogether. How much larger would the audience be if the cutbacks in shortwave had not occurred?

The research shows us that despite the growth of other platforms, most people listen to international radio through the old-fashioned medium of shortwave. This situation is likely to continue unless the major international radio stations make further unwise and unjustified cuts.

What are the main factors that lead people around the world to seek out international radio stations like the Voice of America, BBC, Radio

France Internationale, and others? A few years ago, I compared audience levels for the BBC with various major social, political, and communications indicators. I found that with only two exceptions, the BBC gained large audiences only in countries with a state monopoly and little listening choice. This analysis used data from 1992, but I believe that you would get similar results today. When people have limited information available to them they will look for alternatives. The BBC, the VOA, RFA, Radio France Internationale, Deutsche Welle, and other international broadcasters may provide what audiences are looking for and make it available via the only medium that can reliably reach them: shortwave. It is very important that they continue to do so.

Of course, there is no guarantee that people living in places where the media are not free will inevitably become listeners to international radio. There are countries with state monopolies of information where the BBC audience is nonetheless very small. Programs have to be attractive; they must be in appropriate languages; they must provide the kinds of information that listeners are seeking; they have to offer something not available elsewhere, especially on domestic media. Given options, most people in the world will choose a domestic radio or TV station, provided that the content is high-quality and of interest. They tune to international stations when they find something lacking in available domestic media.

There have been huge changes in control of media over the past fifteen or so years. In 1990, most of the world's electronic media were tightly controlled by governments. In that year, in the fifty-three countries in Africa, for example, virtually all radio and TV stations (with only minor exceptions) were run by the state. Now there are several hundred private radio stations and at least a hundred private TV stations. The same has been seen in the former Soviet Union and in most other former communist countries and in much of Asia. But these developments in deregulation are only just beginning in the Arab world. In some Arab countries there is no movement at all. There are several countries where the state remains dominant over all media: Mauritania, Libya, Syria, Saudi Arabia, Yemen, Iran, Chad, Zimbabwe, Rwanda, Laos, Vietnam, Burma, Turkmenistan, and Belarus are just a few examples. Audience research is not possible in all these countries, but where it is, it shows conclusively that audiences for international radio on shortwave remain large.

Often I am asked, "Do audiences still listen to shortwave?" It is the wrong question. People don't listen to radio defined by the Herzian waves that they use. Shortwave is merely a means of delivery. And to many people in the world, it is the normal means by which they listen to any radio. This is especially true in poor rural areas of Africa. People tune to programs that they choose to listen to or watch; they don't listen because of the medium that provides the content. People will use whatever technology or means of delivery is necessary for them to obtain what they are seeking.

During the 1990s, before the end of the military dictatorship in Nigeria, a survey in Northern Nigeria showed that the BBC had a higher weekly reach there than it achieved even in the UK. At that time, Nigerians had local FM radio services. Despite growing access

The research shows us that despite the growth of other platforms, most people listen to international radio through the old-fashioned medium of shortwave. This situation is likely to continue unless the major international radio stations make further unwise and unjustified cuts.

to FM, they still listened in huge numbers to the BBC entirely on shortwave. Today, despite some limited deregulation, audiences for the BBC, Deutsche Welle, and VOA remain large in Nigeria, especially in the north, where Hausa is spoken. If the BBC, VOA, and other broadcasters also began to broadcast in other Nigerian languages like Yoruba and Ibo, audiences in that country would be very much larger.

News and related content is the main attraction for most listeners. However, the BBC has been very successful, in Africa especially, in providing a program range of sport, drama, arts, debate, listener participation programs, and features on health (particularly on HIV/AIDS and malaria), development challenges, and education. The growth of the cell phone has enabled listeners to send text messages to the BBC. The cell phone has made it possible and relatively inexpensive for listeners from many poor countries to text international broadcasters and their responses can be aired within minutes of being sent.

With the rapid deregulation of broadcasting in so much of the world, the VOA, Radio France Internationale, BBC, and others have put much effort— and quite a lot of money—into FM relays and rebroadcasts on local stations. These efforts are worthwhile, important, and effective. However, there are several problems that need to be considered. FM relays and rebroadcasts are subject to local regulation and the sudden intervention of governments. Nigeria has stopped all local rebroadcasts and relays. The Ivory Coast government stopped all foreign broadcasts on local stations and relays for a while during the recent conflict. Congo Kinshasa, Uzbekistan, Azerbaijan, and several other countries have taken similar actions. In such circumstances, only shortwave can overcome all local regulation and controls.

Is the Internet, as some have said, "the shortwave of the twenty-first century"? This is an interesting and in many ways useful idea. It is true that the Internet crosses boundaries of politics and can reach people in countries where there are restrictions on normal mainstream media such as the radio, TV, or the press. But the analogy is partial and misleading. The Internet can be blocked far more easily than shortwave. The Internet is accessible only to those who have a computer and access to a phone line or other means of connection, or to those who use Internet cafes regularly. Many Internet users in the world today use it solely for sending emails. They do not use it to access news or other sources of information; they cannot afford to do so. This economic barrier to Internet use is certain to increase as Web sites become ever more content-heavy and ever less designed with those who use slow dial-up connections in mind.

Shortwave radio is probably the only way by which we can all be sure of being able to access information at any time and in any place without worrying about permission, or cost, or connectivity, or bandwidth, or having the right antenna or several other complex technological concerns that we hear increasingly. Shortwave is still a relevant and very modern medium for twenty-first century communication. John Tusa, Director of the BBC World Service from 1986 to 1992, foresaw the problem that we see today, that shortwave would be downgraded or disregarded. With all the new technology it was always likely that the old would be seen as past or out of date. Tusa made the important point that if shortwave had been discovered in the 1980s, we would be astonished and greatly attracted to what it had to offer. No other delivery mechanism is capable of sending material over huge distances without interference and at virtually no cost to the receiver. No other medium has the universality of shortwave.

Alan Heil, in his book on the Voice of America, quotes international broadcasting scholar and Middle East specialist Douglas Boyd as citing four principal reasons that "nations broadcast to others." Boyd says that these are to enhance international prestige, to promote national interests, to attempt religious or political indoctrination, or to foster cultural ties.[1] These may well be the reasons that governments or others provide funds for international broadcasting, but I don't recognize any of these motives in any of the very many people I know who work in international radio. The only reasons to broadcast are to communicate, to inform, to provide a service, and to share something worthwhile, true, interesting, entertaining, or enlightening. When the VOA first broadcast in 1942, it said, "The news may be good for us. The news may be bad. But we will tell you the truth."[2] That is all that matters. Everything else is propaganda.

Notes

1.   Alan L. Heil Jr., *Voice of America: A History* (New York: Columbia University Press, 2003), 4.

2.   *Ibid.*, 32.

5. VOICE OF AMERICA IN CHINA

Paul P. Blackburn

LET ME START with a candid admission: although I think surrogate radio has an important role to play in international broadcasting, my strongest affections belong to the Voice of America (VOA). I have felt a strong affinity for VOA since the days I relied on it for news in villages in northeast Thailand and throughout Africa, listened to it in cities all around the world, and discussed its content with listeners in many, many countries. I particularly remember my experiences in China, where both ordinary citizens and Communist Party "America-watchers" told me how much they appreciated the VOA and would cite specific broadcasts of direct interest to them. Another early influence was my first public affairs officer, Jack O'Brien, author of the VOA charter in 1960 and one of its most ardent champions. Then, in 1968, I briefly worked in the VOA newsroom under the lash of chief-editor Bernie Kamenske, and I got an indelible lesson in what it means to apply the highest professional standards to every single news item prepared for broadcast.

Later, during the Carter administration, as the chief of USIA's fast guidance unit, I was the gatekeeper—the firewall, if you will—between VOA and the rest of the bureaucracy during that uneasy period when commentaries, soon to become identified as official editorials, were imposed on a very reluctant VOA.

Let me make four main points about the present. First, VOA is an essential ingredient in the U.S. public diplomacy mix. In its own independent fashion, it serves the same purposes as embassy media relations, speaker programs, and those "last three feet" contacts at our posts on the

Since retiring in 2002 from a forty-year career in the Foreign Service, Paul P. Blackburn has worked part-time for the State Department as a Freedom of Information reviewer. In 2006, he produced www.usdiplomacy.org, a new multimedia Web site of the Association for Diplomatic Studies and Training (ADST) on the history and current practice of American diplomacy.

ground out in the field. At a time when the United States is fighting an
unpopular war and faces heavy criticism around the world, even from our
friends, and when opinion leaders in every nation are hungry for news and
analysis about our policies and purposes and the deeper currents in our
society, it is imperative that we maintain and strengthen this fixed asset.
That we're proposing to cut our English broadcasting at such a critical
juncture represents an appalling failure to advance U.S. long-term foreign
policy interests. If we aspire to continuing global leadership, how can we
even consider retrenchment of our worldwide English broadcasts, especially
at a time when stations like Al Jazeera English and the English service of
Radio China International are broadcasting in English 24/7?

Second, "VOA" is a credibility brand, one whose reputation has
been painstakingly built over many decades. As such it is a jewel worth
cherishing and exploiting. Don't let it suffer the fate of U.S. Information
Service (USIS) offices, now replaced in our embassies by Public Affairs
Sections. Though the function is similar, the new terminology suggests
rigid bureaucracy and carries little of the cachet among foreign publics
earned by many a USIS office. Like the Fulbright exchange program,
the International Visitor Leadership Program, and our more recent
information resource centers, and like USIS before we casually tossed that
brand onto the trash heap in 1999, the very name VOA bespeaks a society
that is open, candid, and welcoming, one that is prepared to offer peoples
of other countries a full, fair picture of America. No surrogate service or
Radio Sawa can possibly do the same.

Third, VOA broadcasting to China in English or in Chinese deserves
very high priority not just during crises like the 1989 Tiananmen tragedy or
the aftermath of our 1999 accidental bombing of the Chinese embassy in
Belgrade, but day in and day out. Key target audiences listen to the English
broadcasts, now mostly Special English broadcasts, while the excellent
programming of the Mandarin and other Chinese services manages daily
to overcome serious obstacles and reach millions via radio, TV satellite
broadcasting, the Internet and massive email distribution. These broadcasts
touch a Chinese audience unequalled in enthusiasm for "American studies."
Whether they like us, fear us, want to exploit us, hope to make money from
us, or aspire to join the 62,000 Chinese students now on our campuses,
nearly every Chinese believes his or her future is somehow tied up with the
strange, powerful nation called the United States.

Fourth, we should take VOA seriously, and stop subjecting it to the
death of a thousand cuts. Despite the need, the vast opportunities and
its capacity for delivering a product that admirably serves U.S. interests,
VOA appears to the outside eye an institution in eclipse, especially when

viewed from the perspective of funding levels requested and amounts appropriated. Why is this happening? Partly it is because of the stronger political appeal of Radio Free Asia (RFA) and other harder-edged surrogate broadcasting services that address specific short-term purposes. But an equally important factor, I believe, is that the BBG, the Congress, and much of our professional diplomatic service seem to have lost respect for the VOA approach to broadcasting.

> If we aspire to continuing global leadership, how can we even consider retrenchment of our worldwide English broadcasts, especially at a time when stations like Al Jazeera English and the English service of Radio China International are broadcasting in English 24/7?

When serving as Director of the Public Diplomacy Office in the Bureau of East Asian and Pacific Affairs until 2002, I found scant support in my bureau or elsewhere in the State Department—outside public diplomacy circles—for the VOA charter's principles that its news really should be "accurate, objective, and comprehensive," or that it should include "responsible discussions and opinions" alongside official statements. Rare indeed is the non-public diplomacy State Department employee who has ever visited VOA, much less soaked up the "Teachings of Bernie Kamenske" in the VOA newsroom.

I will close with three examples from my time as public affairs officer in China in 1997-2000 to illustrate how, funding levels aside, we manage to shoot ourselves in the foot by short-changing VOA.

1. Although consistently mentioned in our annual Human Rights report on China, we have for many years chosen not to make an issue with the PRC of Chinese jamming VOA and RFA broadcasts or blocking their Internet sites.

2. Reflecting unhappiness with VOA's decision in 1997, over White House objections, to broadcast an interview with released dissident Wei Jingsheng, my embassy elected not to push the Chinese to allow stationing of a Mandarin Service correspondent in Beijing. One was finally sent in 2004, but this useful assignment could have come much earlier.

3. Delivering VOA by powerful AM/FM direct broadcast to China from nearby countries is both desirable and technically feasible. Unfortunately, because the BBG at that time placed higher priority on RFA, which was anathema to the Chinese, than on VOA, whose broadcasts were of much less concern,

third-country discussions involving both institutions in a single package became needlessly complicated and therefore less likely to produce outcomes beneficial to VOA broadcasting.

Despite such concerns, we must never lose sight of the essential fact that VOA broadcasts to China and the rest of the world remain critically important to America's national interest. Let's shine up the VOA jewel and once more wear it with pride and purpose.

PART 3
PROGRAMMING

6. RENAISSANCE

Sanford J. Ungar

THERE IS RICH IRONY in the fact that the United States seemed to communicate better with the outside world during the Cold War than it does today. In those bad old days, when nuclear war sometimes appeared to be imminent and the Communist bloc routinely assaulted the West with heavy-handed propaganda, Americans, as a people, were somehow able to exhibit a calm confidence about ourselves and participate in, even sponsor, cool-headed conversations about the strengths and weaknesses of our own system.

There was, for one thing, a network of American Centers around the world, attached to and yet distinct from U.S. embassies and consulates, with the mission of communicating the essence of American culture and society in myriad ways. Young people used the libraries of these centers to peruse college catalogues and investigate places where they might study in the United States, or just to read the lively and sometimes outrageous back-and-forth in American magazines and journals about the events of the day. Audiences of all ages turned out for concerts, symposia, art exhibits, film screenings, and theater productions.

From my travels as a journalist, editor, and lecturer, I can conjure up images of golden moments over several decades: a heated debate in Paris, in the midst of a U.S. presidential election cycle, about the future of the American two-party system; a Los Angeles theater group's visit to Bratislava, which became the occasion for dissidents to emerge from isolation and mingle improbably with people they otherwise never could have met; open arguments, during the worst moments of apartheid in South Africa, about whether or not the lessons of civil rights struggles in the United States were relevant to that country's future.

One of my most vivid memories comes from the late 1970s on the island of Zanzibar, a virtual hothouse at the time for disputes over the merits

Sanford J. Ungar, a veteran print and broadcast journalist, was director of the Voice of America from June 1999 through June 2001. He is now president of Goucher College in Baltimore.

of various models of economic and political development. The Soviet and Chinese consulates, situated on opposite sides of the same street, were busily making utter fools of themselves with their rival photo displays and crude loudspeaker attacks on each other over the Ussuri River incident of a decade earlier, which had contributed to the notorious Sino-Soviet split.

Meanwhile, the funky and minimally staffed U.S. consulate there stood above the fray and sponsored genuine and calm conversations on the international issues of the day, and it was a thrill to drop in and participate. Perhaps I was hopelessly naïve, but as far as this visitor could tell, in the nooks and crannies of Zanzibar, as in Paris or Bratislava or Cape Town or, one could only suppose, many other places around the world, no one was overtly keeping track of who was scoring points against whom during these sessions or how much each event was contributing to a potential victory in the war on anything. The business of the day was simply to demonstrate the exciting, if messy, complexity of American life and letters. It was appealing to all who took part, and stood in stark contrast to the way that others were conducting themselves.

At the same time, overseas publics (including government officials and intellectuals) were avidly listening to the Voice of America (VOA), taking in straightforward news about the United States and the rest of the world, learning and practicing English, and being inspired by, among other things, the jazz programs of Willis Conover, one of the best-known Americans anywhere. The music he played and the interviews he conducted, it was often said, helped people realize that American-style improvisation and innovation were just possibly more inspiring than an overdeveloped sense of order and discipline. And the information in the news and feature programs on VOA was particularly trustworthy because it came from one of the world's most reliable and skilled correspondent corps.

I did not especially know the term at the time, but I suppose all of this constituted "public diplomacy" at its best. There was a charm and an innocence to it, perhaps, but it worked; it helped people everywhere identify with and understand better the American people. Of course issues like Vietnam and Watergate loomed large, but the domestic dissent and turmoil over these matters were obvious to all and, like the civil rights movement of an earlier time, probably appreciated as symptoms of a healthy democracy. It was not that the competition with the Soviets or anyone else was suspended, or that the United States gave up on its Cold War struggle to win friends and influence people, but the communication was straightforward and subtle, rather than overbearing.

Many years later, I had the privilege of serving for two years as President Bill Clinton's last director of VOA. This was a so-called reform era, when a new Broadcasting Board of Governors (BBG), a bipartisan group of private citizens, was established to serve as a firewall to protect VOA and other American international broadcasters from political interference. With the American libraries and cultural centers around the world, as well as many small consulates, long since closed—victims of cuts in the foreign affairs budget based on the conceit that the United States had "won" the Cold War and no longer needed to worry about promoting itself, and of an absorption of the U.S. Information Agency into the State Department—the Voice of America may have become symbolically more important than ever.

The reality, alas, was something else: most members of Congress vacillated between indifference or hostility toward VOA; many acknowledged freely that they did not even know where its headquarters was (practically within shouting distance of the Rayburn House Office Building) or readily confused it with Radio Free Europe/Radio Liberty (RFE/RL), by then based in Prague. Certain key staff members on Capitol Hill, convinced that VOA was an unnecessary relic of the past and a cumbersome bureaucracy to boot, did everything they could to cut VOA's budget and otherwise make it harder for the network to function. As for the BBG, most of its members traveled widely, played VOA and RFE/RL and the other broadcast networks (Radio Free Asia and the Office of Cuba Broadcasting) off against each other during their two- or three-day monthly meetings, and told anyone who would listen how important their new government "agency" was.

The real problems began when the BBG embarked upon "language service review." On paper, the review was a laudable effort to eliminate overlapping broadcasts from different radios, identify countries where meaningful progress had been made toward open media, and establish rational priorities for the use of scarce resources. The first decisions were relatively easy and mostly logical: cutting or ending broadcasts, for example, to the Baltic states and other nations that were progressing toward membership in NATO or the European Union. Before long, however, on the basis of flimsy "research" and questionable audience surveys, the BBG and its staff were proposing to do away with broadcasts to hotspots like Turkey and Thailand, and—to the astonishment of practically every professional broadcaster in the world—to first diminish and then extinguish its signature news service in English. In the lingo of the BBG, English was no longer a "priority one" language for U.S. international broadcasting. Instead, the languages to be emphasized were those that could make a distinct contribution to the "war on terror." As the Board became more ideological in its orientation, there was a temptation to try to use this newly discovered radio weapon to help the military effort in Iraq and Afghanistan.

For a U.S. government–run broadcast network to be silent in English is, of course, absurd. As important as it may be in today's world for Americans to become conversant with other languages, millions of people around the world still strive to learn English, and especially its American variant, in order to be well informed, to study, and to do business.

Listeners who cannot locate English on VOA easily find plenty of other places to go for English-language programs, including Middle Eastern networks that the U.S. government considers anathema.

Beyond that, there is the obvious issue that every country must represent itself in its own language; so long as anyone is listening, the impact is symbolically important. Whatever their surveys might tell them about audience numbers, the people who run Radio France Internationale would never think of not broadcasting in French; nor would Radio Moscow abandon broadcasts in Russian, or Radio Beijing in Chinese. Listeners who cannot locate English on VOA easily find plenty of other places to go for English-language programs, including Middle Eastern networks that the U.S. government considers anathema.

One can scarcely tune in to VOA English on the radio dial in the Middle East these days because there have been severe cuts in VOA transmissions to the region (not to mention the replacement of the VOA Arabic service by commercial-style broadcasts). Furthermore, English scripts have long been the essential building blocks for the other forty-four languages at VOA; these services rely on solid, carefully sourced newscasts provided by a central English news center to produce full service programs of global scope and the highest quality. This resource is now threatened.

Emergency fixes to postpone the demise of English and other key language broadcasts, such as the one obtained during the 2007 congressional budget process through lobbying by a bipartisan coalition of former VOA directors and long-time career employees, are clearly temporary and inadequate.

If anything, a renaissance of the Voice of America is desperately needed. On radio (disseminated by traditional shortwave signals, where necessary, as well as on FM affiliate stations), television, and the Internet, VOA must demonstrate itself anew to be a model American journalistic enterprise, providing news and features from an independent perspective that reflect the complexity of American life, as called for in the charter approved by Congress in 1976. Any taint of promoting government policies must be removed once again; the current heavy-handed "editorials" reflecting official views cannot be allowed to compete with straightforward reporting from the field.

There will always be a certain contradiction inherent in the very existence of an independent, feisty news organization sustained and sponsored by the U.S. government. But if it is properly nurtured and returned to its essential purpose, it can be stronger and more effective in the years ahead.

7. Conversation With America

Myrna Whitworth

"AMERICAN TRADITIONS and the American ethic require us to be truthful, but the most important reason is that truth is the best propaganda and lies are the worst. To be persuasive we must be believable; to be believable we must be credible; to be credible we must be truthful. It is as simple as that."[1]

With those words in 1963, then U.S. Information Agency Director Edward R. Murrow fully expressed the guiding principles that had been implicit in the work of the Voice of America (VOA) since its first broadcast in the opening days of World War II.

However, geopolitically the world looks very different today than it did during World War II and the Cold War that followed. International terrorism, globalization, rising nationalism, and a single global superpower now dominate *after* the collapse of the Soviet Union in 1991 and the horrific events of 9/11 ten years later. The international media environment also is becoming increasingly competitive as people have more choices for news and information transmitted on a variety of media. While remaining faithful to its core principles, the challenge for U.S. international broadcasting today is to develop programming and transmission strategies that are relevant to the audience and a offer a better understanding of the United States and its people.

No matter what the transmission strategy, whether it is the new media of Internet, traditional shortwave, or FM and television relays, international broadcasting is uniquely positioned to carry on a *real time* interactive dialogue—a conversation—with the peoples of the world focusing on what we have in common and allowing for a critical and honest evaluation of our differences. Programming and formats must be designed to attract the movers and shakers of today and those who are being groomed to lead tomorrow. But they must also appeal to a more diverse demographic,

---

Myrna Whitworth, a twenty-eight year veteran of the Voice of America, served as acting director of the agency on three separate occasions, including in the summer and fall of 2001. At the time of her retirement in 2002, she was VOA program director.

including the young discontented, especially in the Muslim world, women, students, and even children.

If at the highest levels, the United States government follows a policy of limited or no official diplomatic discourse, it makes it all the more imperative for a concerted public diplomacy effort using soft power to open and sustain a dialogue with the citizens of the world.

The conversation becomes more critical when the U.S. administration is reluctant to engage in a dialogue with adversarial governments and organizations. If at the highest levels, the United States government follows a policy of limited or no official diplomatic discourse, it makes it all the more imperative for a concerted public diplomacy effort using soft power to open and sustain a dialogue with the citizens of the world. Given the country's image problem, the task will not be easy. Anti-Americanism is on the rise and has become a global phenomenon. The Pew Global Attitudes Project, which has documented this rise since 2002, attributes most of the animosity to U.S. foreign policy: the war in Iraq, the war on terrorism, unilateralism, and unrivaled power. Today, however, the American people also are being viewed more negatively and characterized by such terms as "greedy, violent, and dishonest."[2]

Perhaps these impressions are not surprising given the picture of American life and culture portrayed in the myriad American commercial films, television programs, and pop music in the global marketplace. While the United States is still the country most people want to visit, study in, and live in, and America is still respected for its technology, work ethic, rule of law, and civil liberties, recent polls suggest that there is concern that America and its popular culture are threatening to overwhelm traditional values and ways of life. All the more reason for a full-service international broadcaster that will engage in an open and honest conversation with the world about all aspects of the United States, its policies, its people and its culture. Nowhere is this more critical than in the Middle East.

To reach the Arab World, the Broadcasting Board of Governors (BBG) convinced Congress and the Bush administration to replace the VOA brand, trained journalists, and substantive programming with the 24/7 Radio Sawa network and the Alhurra Television Service. These were created at considerable taxpayer expense to blanket the Middle East with easily replicated music play lists, "news light" and low-impact television that cannot compete with the sophistication and variety offered by other channels to the region. As several recent studies have suggested, Radio Sawa and Alhurra Television give lip service to high journalistic standards, but have not followed them. Radio Sawa, intended to appeal to the youths of the Arab street, should be the perfect vehicle to generate critical dialogue among young people in the United States and in the Arab World on such diverse topics as pop culture, shared values, and life styles. Instead, the American voice to Middle East youth has been guilty of reinforcing the negative stereotypes by broadcasting songs with such lyrics as "He's nothing but a pimp," and "I'm going to let you have your way with me." For its part, according the many speakers of Arabic who have viewed it, Alhurra's often unprofessional and unappealing programs have had minimal impact in the region. Rather than unsuccessfully competing head to head with American commercial channels or with Al Jazeera and Al Arabiya, it should carve out its own niche communicating with the region on topics of mutual interest and importance that are not offered elsewhere.

In *Voice of the New Arab Public: Iraq, al Jazeera and Middle East Politics Today*, Marc Lynch surveyed nearly a thousand Al Jazeera talk shows and found that they focused overwhelmingly on Arab concerns, including Western imperialism, and often from a solely Arab perspective. Lynch quotes Egyptian analyst Magdi Khalil: "The Arab street is cut off from the international street in its concerns and goals ... globalization, the environment, human rights, unemployment, women's rights, freedom of religion, right to development."[3] Dialogue on these issues, and others, discussed from both an American and Arab perspective, should be a key output of both Radio Sawa and Alhurra.

Several years ago, VOA management consulted a group of regional specialists about the role for U.S. broadcasting in the competitive Middle East media market. While they confirmed that comprehensive and credible news from the United States should remain a priority, they stressed the need to find ways to more effectively reach a younger generation of critical thinkers, particularly with programs that permitted an exchange of views with their counterparts in the United States. One idea that came from these consultations was an Americana program hosted by an Arab equivalent of Alistair Cooke that would focus on the diversity and vibrancy of American life and culture. It would seek to look at the United States through Arab eyes and to offer perspectives more complex and subtle than those held by many people in the Middle East.

Our experts also proposed regular "letters from America" on current issues by a rotating series of Arab and Arab-American specialists, offered to reinforce the perception that U.S. international broadcasting is balanced, thus strengthening its credibility. Other initiatives included women's programs that provide an opportunity for a dialogue on issues that concern all women, whether they live in Boston and Denver or Baghdad and

Damascus. These include child rearing, health, and education, as well as life styles and entertainment. Other suggestions: conversations among conflicting parties in the area with locally produced programs focusing on conflict resolution, peace, and dialogue. Interstitial segments should be designed to offer brief insights into American life, culture, thought, and values. Arab-American communities should be tapped and the voices of Arab students studying in the United States should be heard. There is an important role for U.S. international broadcasting to the Middle East; it can tell America's stories, put into context American values and culture, and engage the Arab world in a constructive conversation with the American people, and in the process, be an intelligent alternative to Arabic satellite channels and anti-American rhetoric. Such conversations are imperative; this approach should be replicated worldwide.

Recognizing the need to engage the audience, most of the forty-five language services of the Voice of America are broadcasting radio and television programs that open the dialogue, especially with younger audiences. Interactive programming takes various forms, from discussions on topics that have been selected by the audience through queries received by mail, recorded hotline calls, and emails to live televised and radio call-in shows broadcast regularly in Persian, Indonesian, Urdu, English, Afghan languages, and Mandarin, among others. Many services are addressing youth audiences with programs that focus on culture and life-styles presented by knowledgeable and personable hosts. Youth programs to Afghanistan, Central Africa, Mozambique, Nigeria, Cambodia, Tibet, and Indonesia offer additional segments that facilitate discussion among young people on the issues of peace, reconciliation, and the importance of open communication.

Many of these conversations may be short lived if the Broadcasting Board of Governors has its way. Without a focus on long-range strategic planning rather than short-term tactical needs, the BBG is threatening to eliminate or reduce radio services in a number of critical languages, including Albanian, English, Georgian, Hindi, Serbian, Russian, and Uzbek, among others. VOA services in the post-9/11 world must justify their existence based on two criteria: do they have sufficient audience share, and are they contributing to the "war on terror"? Services that do not meet the criteria are in jeopardy. To guarantee their survival, news, information, and conversations on shared interests and values are giving way to music, soft radio features, and light television fare that can be rebroadcast on local stations. Voice of America is producing over a hundred hours a week of television in twenty-five languages, some of it very good. Television programming that is delivered via satellite directly to audience homes carries breaking news and tackles controversial subjects. However most television productions are designed for local station placement. While some do an excellent job of telling the American story within the context of the audience, many are devoid of news and appear designed not to offend governments where they are rebroadcast. Placement programming, both radio and television, also runs the constant risk of being shut off at the whim of the station or the government. A case in point is Russia, once a lucrative market for both VOA and Radio Free Europe/Radio Liberty rebroadcasts. Today, because of Vladimir Putin's media crackdown, the American voice in Russia is a mere whisper. One can only puzzle at the BBG plan to further silence international broadcasting with the complete elimination of all VOA Russian radio services and shortwave transmissions.

Another service that apparently is not meeting the BBG's two-pronged criteria is VOA English, which until a few years ago was a vibrant 24/7 service that instantly reported and immediately responded to breaking news developments anywhere in the world. Since 2001, the BBG has been chipping away at the English product, relegating it first to a second-tier language and then advocating its total elimination. The Board has turned a deaf ear to protests that English is our national language, is spoken by more than a billion people around the world, and is the international language of commerce, trade, and the Internet. Members have not been swayed by the argument that English shortwave broadcasts are not subject to jamming by such countries as China and Burma, nor that China, Russia, France, Iran, and the Arabic Al Jazeera recognize the importance of English and have increased their English product. The reality is that a good public service broadcaster providing quality content may not draw the numbers that a music channel will. Yet since 2002, the Board of Governors has placed more importance on winning audience share than in conversing with those of influence in societies reached. As a result, the United States has lost many in its traditional, high quality audience: reformers, intellectuals, government leaders, and elites who are critical to effecting change.

But there are ways to have it all. An Internet presence in many of the threatened languages would create interactivity and dialogue between the world and the United States, especially with its young people, at a fraction of the cost of television or even radio. It also would provide a platform should instability or hostility break out and a greater news and information presence is required.

New media already have proven to be powerful. Worldwide terrorist networks use the Web to recruit and instruct. Osama bin Laden once relied on televised videos to disseminate his propaganda; today the Internet is his medium of choice. From Manila to Kuwait city, from Riyadh to Kathmandu, and even in war-torn Congo, cell phones and text messaging networks are changing the way political mobilization is conducted. According to Internet World Stats, nearly one fifth of the world's population is connected in some way to the Internet; that is over 1 billion Internet users worldwide, most in the critical 15-30 year age group, and that figure changes upward every day. For instance, the Middle East has seen a 920 percent increase in Internet use in the past seven years.[4]

And how is international broadcasting addressing the new technology? The platform for delivering the new media is operative, but funding has not been forthcoming for content development. Every year since 2000, Voice of America management has presented the BBG with detailed budget proposals for Internet program funding to be included in Office of Management and Budget submissions. These have not made it past the initial vetting process; VOA has been forced to cobble together its Internet presence from existing funds and with diminished staff in the threatened services, many of whom need training in the new media. Its sister grantees have fared little better.

Voice of America staff and management must be applauded for what they have been able to accomplish. VOA has an Internet presence in all its services, although in most, this amounts to a Web portal for audio and video files on demand, with some live streaming of programs in real time. The English VOANEWS.com remains a popular Web site even though it is staffed only eighteen hours a day. Services provide RSS feeds for some of their programming; many also use email newsletters. News reports to mobile devices are now offered in eleven languages with more coming online every day, and VOA Russian and English are producing three-minute video newscasts for the Internet; other services will join them in 2008. Several programs also are available through podcasts. However, with a staff of 1,200, VOA only has about 30 people working full time to provide Web content. Another 130 people, many of them contract employees, repurpose radio and television content, but few have Internet as part of his or her job requirements, so work on the Internet is performed only if and when other duties are completed. While commendable, VOA still lags behind in developing innovative content that captures the full potential of the new media.

The Internet can inexpensively deliver substantive news and information. But it can do much more. It provides a participatory medium for an open-ended conversation, one that assumes equality among the participants. Through blogs, chat rooms, and networks based on common interests, it encourages peer-to-peer discussion that assumes active players getting to know each other in cyberspace. Simply put, it offers an opportunity for the United States to talk *with* and not *at* the rest of the world, and to do so instantaneously. But it also requires a new way of thinking, a new way of developing and sharing content. And most importantly it requires a serious commitment on the part of the BBG and Congress to factor Internet programming into future budgets.

Voice of America's role is as important today as it was sixty-six years ago. Its core principles and high journalistic standards and values reflect what we are as a country. It must not resort to focusing on ideological differences in a war of ideas or become a megaphone concentrating so heavily on U.S. government policy in its "war on terror" that it loses its credibility. Instead, with a minimum of reorganization and resource reallocation, it has an opportunity to create a much-expanded dialogue with the world and to foster partnerships based on mutual respect.

Notes

1. Edward R. Murrow, testimony before Congress, May 1963.

2. *America's Image in the World: Findings from the Pew Global Attitudes Project.* Testimony of Andrew Kohut, president, Pew Research Center, before the Subcommittee on International Organizations, Human Rights and Oversight Committee on Foreign Affairs, U.S. House of Representatives, March 14, 2007.

3. Marc Lynch, *Voice of the New Arab Public: Iraq, al Jazeera and Middle East Politics Today* (New York: Columbia University Press, 2006), 79.

4. Internet World Stats: Usage and Population Statistics, September 2007, www.internetworldstats.com/stats5.html/. Accessed November 25, 2007.

8. The Continuing Crucial Mission of Radio Free Europe/Radio Liberty

Jeffrey Trimble

RECENTLY, A MAN NAMED SIARHIEJ SKRABIEC was released from a labor camp in Vitebsk, Belarus, after serving a year and a half as a political prisoner. Skrabiec, a former Belarus parliamentarian, and his campmate, former presidential candidate Alexander Kazulin, who's serving a five-year sentence, had a smuggled shortwave receiver with them in jail, and they regularly tuned in to Radio Free Europe/Radio Liberty (RFE/RL) at six o'clock in the morning to listen to Belarus Service broadcasts.

Immediately after his release, Skrabiec said on air on the Belarus Service: "Alexander Kazulin and I listened to your radio every day in the camp. There are jamming stations, but they're old. I hope that this night, Kazulin will hear my voice on your airwaves. So Alexander, keep it up! I'm doing everything we agreed on. We will win. Thanks so much to all the supporters. Listener calls on Radio Liberty were a great help, as well as solidarity reports on hunger strikes in Warsaw and other places. Thanks to all listeners to Radio Liberty and to all the people who do the broadcasts." Skrabiec was on a call-in show on the Belarus Service on Radio Liberty following his release, and he also joined an online conference.

Crusading Russian journalist Anna Politkovskaya was gunned down outside her Moscow apartment in early October 2006. Her final media appearance two nights before her death was on a Radio Liberty roundtable program in Moscow in which Politkovskaya talked about her latest investigative reporting on the torture by Russian authorities of detainees in Chechnya. She was killed before these articles even were published in her newspaper, *Novaya Gazeta*, but she had spoken about the subject matter on Radio Liberty. I cite these instances as sober, sad reminders that for all the changes that have taken place since the end of the Cold War in RFE/RL's broadcast region, much remains depressingly the same, including control

---

Jeffrey Trimble is director of programming at the Broadcasting Board of Governors. This chapter is based on a speech he delivered in November, 2006, when he was acting president of Radio Free Europe/Radio Liberty.

of speech and independent media. In some instances, Turkmenistan, for instance, repression of human rights, including free speech, has only grown worse. In October, Olgulsapar Muradova, a correspondent of RFE/RL, died in prison in Turkmenistan after being thrown in jail for work she was doing for us and for human rights groups in Turkmenistan.

What are the best programming techniques to reach a universe of differing demographics and information needs today? The answer is that the style and techniques of RFE/RL broadcasting span a wide spectrum that reflects the uneven state of democracy and civil society in our broadcast region.

First, a quick look at RFE/RL today. It is an organization whose internal demographics perhaps would surprise some Cold War veterans. Of our twenty-eight broadcast languages, nineteen are to countries whose populations are primarily Muslim. This reflects the growth in services to those areas and the closure of broadcast services to Central and Eastern Europe and the Baltics in recent years. Another trend is that RFE/RL has diversified and spread its newsgathering operation increasingly into the broadcast region itself, consistent with the Broadcasting Board of Governors strategic plan that calls for broadcasters to gather news and relay programs locally where it is possible to do so. That presents many challenges to us.

Radio Free Europe/Radio Liberty operates twenty-two bureaus throughout our broadcast region, a network of about 1,500 freelancers, and has local contributors throughout the region. All this is managed from our headquarters in Prague, to which we moved in 1995. In October, 2006, we had a groundbreaking ceremony for a relocated headquarters building for RFE/RL, a manifestation of the commitment of Congress and the administration to RFE/RL's continuing mission. That building should be ready by the end of 2008.

I want to emphasize that our product, as all of those in U.S. international broadcasting, is research-driven. We do everything that we possibly can to first identify target audiences, and then determine the best way—given resources and our ability to reach audiences—to get the messages out to the target audiences. This is an absolutely crucial point. The programming spectrum in which RFE/RL operates today crosses roughly three environments: (1) those where repression is the state of play, such as Belarus, Turkmenistan, and Iran; (2) the relatively open and rich media environments, such as Serbia, Ukraine, and Iraq; and (3) the gray areas, where people have access to a wide variety of media, and often where they feel well informed, but in fact they aren't because there are black spots where the domestic media don't go, topics they don't cover. The prime example of this is Russia, where electronic media are almost completely dominated by the Kremlin.

So the style and the content of RFE/RL programming is affected by where in the spectrum of media environments our target audience or target country falls. In the more open media markets, we look for ways to add value, to touch on issues in ways that the domestic media are not capable of doing or are not doing for various reasons. I give as an example the time we closed our Baltic services several years ago. In vibrant, open media environments, their listenership was in fact higher than it had ever been. It hurt to shut them down, because listeners still felt they were adding value in those societies. In heavily repressed societies, we tell people truths and give them information about what's happening first and foremost within their own countries, information denied to them by their domestic media outlets. The intermediate markets sometimes are the most difficult, because audiences there sometimes don't appreciate the value added that they can get from RFE/RL products. We see this to some extent in Russia, where, as noted above, people feel—at times mistakenly—that they're relatively well informed by Russian domestic media.

The method of delivery of programming also makes a big difference in the kind of programming that we shape and do. When we can get in-country delivery on local FM radio, we do programming that fits into what increasingly are sophisticated production and presentation techniques in the domestic media market. Programming for cross-border broadcasting, whether on medium wave or still on shortwave, while rich in content, is somewhat simpler in style because of the difficulty of hearing it if you have reception problems, or in the case of Iran, where there is jamming.

We at RFE/RL are actively pursuing a multiple media strategy to take advantage of new and popular platforms to spread the messages. Television is, of course, the preferred medium for news and information almost everywhere in our broadcast region. It's very difficult for us to get access to television. We have entered into a half dozen partnerships in countries where we jointly produce programming that is branded RFE/RL, yet over which we have editorial control. Satellite television is not realistic for RFE/RL because we do not have our own facilities to be able to produce programming and then to get it up on the satellite. It is a very expensive proposition and something we would like to pursue.

Increasingly, and where feasible, we are pursuing the delivery of news and information on hand-held devices, via short message service (text messaging) or Internet-based technologies, for instance. We don't have a Web site in the Turkmen language at this time because Internet usage in Turkmenistan is so low and access to Internet is very difficult. Our Russian language site, however, is new, vibrant, exciting, interactive, and very popular. And in fact, given the difficulty of domestic distribution in Russia, our future there lies primarily in Internet-driven news and information products.

The multimedia approach allows us to promote products across platforms and to present those products in different ways. We might do a relatively brief interview with a subject and then refer listeners repeatedly to the Web site, where they can find full transcripts or longer versions of the interview, where they can get richer content than we're able to give them in limited program time. So you have the multiplier effect for audiences of cross-promotion and usages across these different platforms.

We've had fantastic success on the Internet: regularly, 1.2 million unique visitors a month, and 20 million page views. Television is another way to get the job done, but we are highly vulnerable to the whims of the local authorities any place we do domestic distribution in country. They can take us off the air at any time, and they do so. It happened to us in Ukraine before the last presidential election. It may happen to us and our colleagues at VOA in Russian. So we do accept that there are hazards that are inherent in relying on a strategy, primarily, of domestic distribution.

I'd like to focus just a moment on Radio Farda, our 24/7 broadcast entity to Iran, which has evoked a certain amount of controversy in Washington. We had started Persian broadcasting in 1998; the Broadcasting Board of Governors instructed us to start Radio Farda together with the Voice of America in 2002. The mandate of the station was to attract large audiences, primarily among younger audiences—which, given the population demographic in Iran, is logical—as well as news seekers of all ages. I want to emphasize the inclusion of this last demographic because the station is not just for youths, it is for people who are interested in news and information.

Farda is a success story. In less than four years, it has become the most popular international radio broadcaster in Iran, with a 13.5 percent weekly listenership, compared with BBC in second place, which has 5.6 percent in weekly listenership. Farda carries more news and information daily than any other international radio broadcaster. Under its current schedule, it carries over eight hours of news and information daily, including four thirty-minute news magazines (two produced by our VOA colleagues who sit in RFE/RL offices here in DC, and two produced in Prague). A recent supplemental from Congress has allowed us to enhance Farda's Web site. There is cross promotion between the radio and the Web site, and given that the Iranian authorities jam Farda, we see the Internet as a good way to reach audiences there, although the Iranian authorities have taken steps to restrict and complicate Internet access. But we find that, for the most part, people are still able to access our content.

Finally, some points first made by Gene Parta and Ross Johnson* about why broadcasting was successful during the Cold War. First, there was a clear sense of purpose. Second, there was a sophisticated appraisal of the adversary. Third, we differentiated programming for multiple audiences. Fourth, we broadcast programs that were purposeful, relevant, credible, and responsible. Fifth, we had multiple media operations. Sixth, we had appropriate

> Television is a low-cost way to get the job done, but we are highly vulnerable to the whims of the local authorities any place we do domestic distribution in country. They can take us off the air at any time, and they do so.

funding and oversight operations. Seventh, we maintained distance from official government policies. Finally, we had a receptive audience, many of whom identified with the broadcasters' goals.

Underlying all these points is that surrogate broadcasting—its mission of support of freedom, democracy, and civil society—is not a sprint; it's a marathon. It takes a long time for it to make a real difference and we at RFE/RL are in this race for the long haul.

Editor's note: R. Eugene Parta is head of audience research at Radio Free Europe/Radio Liberty. Ross Johnson is former president of RFE/RL.

9. THE MIDDLE EAST NEWS GAP

Salemeh Nematt

DESPITE GROWING GLOBAL INTEREST in developments in the Middle East and the broader Arab region in the past several years, there continues to be a huge gap in the local, regional, and global media coverage of that part of the world. While the national Arab and Pan-Arab media in the region, predominantly controlled and run by non-democractic Arab governments, continue to practice varying levels of official censorship or self-censorship, international media organizations and the foreign media, including Arabic-language services, have failed to fill the information gap due to a variety of reasons.

The fact that foreign powers such as the United States, France, Britain, Russia, and Germany have established, or are in the process of establishing and launching Arabic-speaking radio and television satellite channels to address this gap is further proof of the existing information deficit caused by the failure of the Arab national and pan-Arab media.

As it stands, Arab public opinion today is shaped by a combination of state-controlled national and pan-Arab media, primarily satellite channels such as the Qatari and Saudi government–owned and -controlled Al Jazeera and Al Arabiya satellite channels respectively, and international news agencies such as the British Reuters, the French Agence France Presse (AFP), and other news services that offer Arabic-language coverage of the region. It goes without saying that local and regional correspondents of these foreign news services are under varying degrees of government influence or outright censorship routinely practiced by the region's governments in respect to local, national, and regional Arab media.

Reuters, one of the world's biggest multimedia news services, is dominant in the region, together with AFP, both of which have a built-

---

As Washington bureau chief for *Al Hayat International Arab* daily (2003-2007), Salemeh Nematt's work focused on reporting and analyzing U.S. foreign policy, including issues related to the war in Iraq, the global war on terrorism, and the U.S. drive for democratization in the broader Middle East, as well as issues related to U.S. military and security strategies in the region.

in anti-American bias. American agencies such as the Associated Press are much less influential in the region. Most Arab newspapers, as well as radio and TV stations, rely on these major agencies for their daily coverage of international and regional developments. The BBC World Service radio and television are arguably among the most globally influential news sources, and they are believed to also have an anti-American bias as evident in a number of scandals involving its editors in the context of the Iraq war coverage and their hostility to the Blair government for its alliance with the United States in that war.

This is not to say that these international news services are unprofessional. But a combination of local government censorship and a built-in anti-American bias result in a less than balanced coverage, which is exacerbated by state-run Arab news media that primarily serve the non-democratic governments in the region rather than the cause of a free press. The fact that the United States is perceived in the region as unfairly backing Israel against the Palestinians and other Arab neighbors further enhances the anti-American bias, not to mention the U.S. invasion and occupation of Iraq, which has not only angered regional governments that control their media, but also heightened anti-American sentiments in Europe.

It is well established that there is a strong sense in Europe, particularly in Britain, France, and Germany, that America, as the world's only superpower and bully, has undermined regional and global security, and in the process, contributed to the rise of political extremism and violence in the region and beyond. Whether this is true or not, the very fact that the United States is widely perceived as such has contributed to the anti-American media coverage on a global level. This, obviously, does not bode well for U.S. public diplomacy in the Arab region or anywhere else for that matter.

Another factor negatively affecting the perception of U.S. policies in the Arab region is the tendency by the Arab media to adopt and reproduce the anti-administration talking points of the U.S. opposition as representative of U.S. policies. As such, the Arab media reproduces what the Democrats say about the incumbent Republican administration as though it were all true, with very little to offset that view from the other side. Under a Democratic administration, the Arab media would adopt the Republican line critical of the administration's policies. The argument is: if this what the Americans say about themselves and their own policies, what are we to say? As a result, torture in Abu Ghraib prison and Guantanamo become the official policy of the United States rather than the exception to the rule that does not permit torture.

I was one of those who got very excited when I heard about U.S. plans to launch Alhurra Arabic-language satellite TV. I wasn't particularly excited about Radio Sawa, in the sense that it was promoting a product that was already popular in the Arab world, entertainment and music. Young people in the Arab world love Brad Pitt and Jennifer Lopez. They have no problems with these cultural icons of America, so packaging them on a radio station that also plays Arabic popular music appeals to them. So Radio Sawa was a hit, a success, as far as pop music is concerned. As far as news is concerned, basically it was picking up the news from the news agencies. They had very little original material per se. I know this, because I was there and I saw how they worked. Which agencies were they picking up? Reuters and AFP of course. I was shocked at one point when Radio Sawa, in order to remain popular with Arab audiences, started to use such terms as "activists" in reference to terrorists, and to "resistance" to describe terrorist attacks in Iraq, which the anti-American, anti-Western media would normally use. At any rate, Radio Sawa succeeded as a pop music channel, but did nothing for American public diplomacy. Hollywood is already in everybody's home in the Arab world; almost everybody loves American movies, everybody loves American culture. The problem is American policy, which comes across as very hostile and very aggressive, and global media coverage enhances this image. I'm not saying there's nothing to blame American policy for; what I'm saying is that it is made much worse than it is already.

So I got excited about Ahurra TV. I remember telling Alhurra's news director at its launch that if he does not get half of his correspondents in the region arrested within three months, then he's not doing his job. The fact is, almost three years since Alhurra came on the air, there was no instance of any correspondent of Alhurra getting in trouble with the authorities. In that part of the world, they don't offer Pulitzer Prizes, but if you get jailed by the authorities, that's your Pulitzer Prize. There is no way you can function properly as a journalist in that region without getting into trouble with the authorities. Alhurra has failed dramatically in this respect. In other words, local Arab media outlets have been much better in challenging the establishment, if you like, than Alhurra.

The statistics I have from 2006 rank Alhurra as fifty-sixth among the top one hundred Arabic satellite channels. We also know that only the top ten satellite channels are of any significance; that is, we know that 90 percent of the audiences regularly watch the top ten channels. Alhurra is almost invisible. Al Arabiya, in contrast, launched at nearly the same time, is now number two—and a very strong number two—to Al Jazeera, compared to Alhurra's ranking of fifty-sixth.

There are many reasons why this happened. Part of the reason is that the people who have been running Alhurra's editorial management were more or less the same people who ran Radio Sawa, and in order to get permission in the Arab countries to broadcast local FM stations for Radio Sawa, they had to get a license. The licenses in these countries have to be approved by the security services, the intelligence services, and you have to be on good terms with these authorities to get that license; you simply had to assure them that you will not broadcast anything that would upset the regime and the political order. The same people who basically agreed to these conditions for Radio Sawa launched Alhurra, and that's why, over the past three years, we saw hardly a single incident of Alhurra creating any kind of serious trouble for any government in the region. Remember, this is a region where torture is in every prison. There are violations of human rights, outright massacres taking place in some countries, such as the massacre of Kurds in Syria in 2005, and routine human rights abuses in Egypt. Have we seen a documentary on Alhurra about how Mubarak's son became so rich? Where did he make his money? How did he maneuver himself to become head of the ruling party's policy planning body and potentially the successor to his father as president? We have not seen a documentary in Al Jazeera about the Qataris kicking out 5,000-6,000 of their own citizens, stripping them of their nationality, and throwing them in the desert. Nobody produced an investigation or a documentary about Reda Hilal, the deputy editor in chief of *Al Ahram*, the leading newspaper in Egypt, who vanished off the face of the earth in 2003. The man just vanished, after repeatedly criticizing his own government and the Islamists in his country. We never found out whatever happened to him.

Almost three years since Alhurra came on the air, there was no instance of any correspondent of Alhurra getting in trouble with the authorities. In that part of the world, there is no Pulitzer Prize, but if you get jailed by the authorities, that's your Pulitzer Prize. There is no way you can function as a journalist without getting into trouble with the authorities. Alhurra has failed dramatically in this respect.

Alhurra, which we hoped would help fill the media vacuum, was not a disaster; it was a blunder. The superpower of the world failed to produce a good television station for the region. The Arab satellite channels today freely cover only two events: The American occupation of Iraq, and the Israeli occupation of Palestine. This is where the Arab media is free to have a field day. But they're not saying anything about what's happening at home in the rest of the Arab countries. Why isn't Alhurra moving in to fill this huge vacuum? I once challenged the news director at a panel on public diplomacy at the American Enterprise Institute: Why wasn't he trying to do the stories that he should be doing to fill the huge news vacuum there? His reply, and I'm paraphrasing, was that he had no mandate to rock the boat and that if he upset the governments of the region, these governments would get on the State Department's case.

U.S. foreign policy in the Middle East today in terms of democracy promotion is unlike U.S. foreign policy in Eastern Europe, where the United States took a stand supporting freedom lovers and reformers. Understandably, rocking the boat in the Arab world could create problems for the U.S. government; there's no question. But with time, these governments will have to realize that they've got to deal with their own information deficit. The United States cannot, in the context of public diplomacy, continue to say it wants to promote democracy in that part of the world when its own Arabic satellite channel does not address these issues. It is ridiculous that in some quarters in the Arab world Alhurra should be called Al Jazeera Lite, the watered-down version of an Arab satellite channel. Corruption and political oppression are occurring on a daily basis in the region. These stories never get covered by the national media. Occasionally you find the BBC covering them. That's why some of these correspondents occasionally are deported or get their visas revoked, and some get arrested. They're doing their job. And some courageous local journalists are also being thrown in jail because they're trying to do their job. Alhurra would have to start doing its job as it should. Either that, or forget about the whole public diplomacy and democracy promotion effort in that region.

10. ALHURRA

Brian T. Conniff

IN A MEDIA ENVIRONMENT in which there are more than 250 satellite television channels, some might ask why the United States needs a TV news and information channel broadcasting to the Middle East. The short answer is that, despite this proliferation of media outlets, there is a shortage of channels that broadcast objective information about the Middle East, the United States, and the world.

Al Jazeera is financed by Qatar; Al Arabiya is backed by Saudi Arabia; and Al Manar is funded by Hezbollah. Each gives its particular slant to the story, a slant seldom critical of those who control the purse strings. In the Arab media world, the presentation of opinion and fact are often so intermingled that it is difficult to distinguish one from the other. Even so-called independent media outlets have government affiliations. Newspaper headlines and top stories on newscasts tout the accomplishments of the ruling party while rarely even mentioning the opposition. Opinion pages and editorials often run on the front page of newspapers, further blurring the distinction between objective facts and biased perspectives. As Middle East political expert Mamoun Fandy recently observed, "Very few Arabs trust newspapers or television to tell them the facts."[1] But Arab audiences are media savvy, and they frequently go to several sources to extract the full story.[2] Alhurra is one such source.

The Executive branch and the Congress agreed that the United States needed to reach out to the people in the region with objective, credible news, instead of relying on local media outlets' interpretations of events or U.S. policy positions. Launched on February 14, 2004, Alhurra was created to broadcast accurate, timely, and relevant news and information about the region, the world, and the United States to a broad Arabic-speaking audience. Although Alhurra is funded by the U.S. government,

Brian T. Conniff is president of the Middle East Broadcasting Networks, Inc. Prior to joining MBN, Mr. Conniff was the executive director of the Broadcasting Board of Governors.

Alhurra is different from state-sponsored or state-influenced Arab media organizations because the legislation that created Alhurra also stipulated that the network (and all international broadcasting) must provide "news which is consistently reliable and authoritative, accurate, objective, and comprehensive." Oversight by the Broadcasting Board of Governors (BBG) allows Alhurra to provide unbiased, professional journalism and to be a model of free press, which is consistent with BBG's aim to uphold the practices of journalism to support freedom, civil society, and democracy.

The healthy skepticism of Arab audiences also leads to their belief that you shouldn't believe anything that you cannot see with your own eyes. We have learned that a news account summarizing a statement by President Bush will not resonate with Arab viewers as much as actual film footage of the president making that statement.[3] Viewers want to see for themselves what the president is saying and to watch his eyes as he says it. It is this need to see things with their own eyes that has led to the rise of satellite news channels in the region. Nowadays, when a reporter talks about a bomb explosion in Israel or fighting in Iraq, television viewers can flip on the television and see it for themselves.

In spite of the proliferation of "news" channels, journalists who speak out and report on human rights violations or corruption in the Middle East often find themselves in jail or, in extreme circumstances, victims of assassination, as was the case with Lebanese journalist Samir Kassir. Even in countries like Egypt, which asserts the existence of a free press, journalists who speak out against local governments are often jailed. In September 2007, four newspaper editors were sentenced to a year of forced labor for "libeling" Egyptian President Hosni Mubarak, to name one example.

Alhurra's journalistic code and its journalists are unique in the region. Many Alhurra journalists moved halfway around the world for the opportunity to work at a television network that operates without government interference. These are talented, dedicated journalists who believe in the value of providing accurate and balanced news coverage to an Arabic-speaking audience. Other differences are seen, in part, in the terms the network uses to report the news. For example, many other Arab networks will use the term "martyr" to describe those Alhurra refers to as "suicide bombers." Al Jazeera and other Arab media outlets condemned the American intervention in Iraq without reporting Saddam Hussein's atrocities; they use phrases such as the "American war on Iraq" and "occupied Iraq" in their daily reporting. Alhurra uses simply "Iraq." Arab news outlets purport to show several sides to a story by, for example, providing footage of Arabs suffering at the hand of Israelis followed by footage of Arabs suffering at the hands of the United States. In contrast, Alhurra broadcasts debates between Arabs and Israelis, Americans and Arabs, and between Arabs with differing points of view. For example, the first time an Israeli official and a pro-government Saudi intellectual appeared together on the same television program was on Alhurra's flagship talk show, *Free Hour*. On March 15, 2007, Miri Eisen, Spokesperson for the Israeli Prime Minister, and Dr. Zouhair El Harthi, a Saudi author and political analyst, discussed the Arab Peace Initiative. They were joined by Nabil Amr, Consultant to the Palestinian President, and Michael Pelletier, U.S. State Department's Media Liaison Officer in Dubai.

At times, Arab news networks let emotion influence the news, and while they may not have started the fire, they certainly fanned the flames in an extremely volatile region.[4] Hugh Miles documented several examples of reporting that seemed designed to incite—rather than to inform—viewers. One such example is that Al Jazeera's repeated broadcast of a clip of the shooting of Muhammad al-Durra, whose death became the network's emblem of the Intifada, and which had a deeply galvanizing effect on the wider Arab public.[5]

In contrast, Alhurra viewers get the facts so they can make their own judgments. Alhurra gives viewers the opportunity to hear all sides of a discussion, including the all-important voice of moderation. The challenge for any network broadcasting to the Middle East is to find a way to stand out from the pack. Each channel needs to find its own niche and a reason for viewers to seek it out amidst the vast array of satellite viewing options. Alhurra is fortunate to have an edge over other regional broadcasters in its ability to cover America, its people, and its policies better and more thoroughly than any other Arabic-language news and information network in the region. It should be noted that Alhurra is not the voice of this administration or any U.S. administration. Rather, its programming presents accurate news and information about the Middle East, the United States, and the world. Through the network's hard news programs and softer cultural offerings, Alhurra provides a personal view of Americans, their participation in the democratic process, and their cultural diversity.

While Alhurra provides news and information in a straightforward manner, it is also able to challenge certain regional or national taboos that other networks cannot. Alhurra is the place where viewers know they can find discussions on human rights, democracy, freedom of speech and the press, and the rights of women. Alhurra is currently the only network to have a program dedicated to the rights of women. Each week the program *Equality* (or *Musawat*), hosted by Nadine Al-Bdair, features expert guests to discuss topics such as the rights of women in Islam, a woman's right to vote, and arranged marriages. Anecdotal research shows that *Equality* is one of Alhurra's most popular programs. And if emails to Alhurra are any indication, this program elicits strong reaction from both men and women. Our female viewers love this program and thank us for having it on. Some male viewers call it blasphemous, yet can recount almost every word that is said on *Equality*. Alhurra has several programs that highlight the values not just of Americans, but also of people around the world, regardless of religion or nationality. At Alhurra, we are free to discuss any topic, whereas other networks in the region are limited by concerns about offending their backers.

> **Alhurra gives viewers the opportunity to hear all sides of a discussion, including the all-important voice of moderation.**

When it comes to American politics, the upcoming presidential election, and our own vigorous debates about the war, health care, and other domestic issues, Alhurra has a distinct advantage. Alhurra provides the most comprehensive U.S. election coverage in the Middle East. But Alhurra also leads in providing coverage of elections in the Middle East. It was the first channel to produce and air televised electoral debates between the candidates in Iraq. Leading up to the 2005 Parliamentary elections in Egypt, popular pan-Arab newspaper *Al-Quds Al-Arabi* stated that "Alhurra television emerged like a black stallion in this satellite competition, since it is able to attract normal viewers and activists alike, thanks to its wide range of guests from the opposition who are not fearful of criticizing the Mubarak regime."[6] Alhurra's electoral coverage often surpasses that of the local channels. For example, in September 2007, Alhurra broadcast more than fifteen hours of live continuous coverage from Morocco during its parliamentary elections. Moroccans tuned into Alhurra because its coverage went beyond the election results to include analysis about the impact the results would have on the nation and the region. Through extensive election coverage and analysis, Alhurra emphasizes the role of personal responsibility in the election process and the impact of free and fair elections.

Alhurra also opens the doors for Arabic language viewers from throughout the Middle East and Europe to see that America is more than the last statement from the White House. The network is in the unique position to highlight the similarities between the United States and the Arab world as well as the differences. Recently, Alhurra produced two program series examining the American experience. The first was a documentary series called *Americans* that highlighted a different aspect of American life and American history in each episode. *Americans* received critical acclaim in the Arabic press. In 2006, *Al-Hayat* newspaper wrote:

The opportunity for an Arab journalist to cover and film the United States of America is a rare commodity in our media institutions. But Alhurra TV offered that opportunity to Ephrem Kossaify (host of *Americans*). One of Alhurra's missions is to present America to Arab spectators, and it seems that Kossaify seized that opportunity in a way no other journalist in Alhurra or in most of other Arab TV channels did. We can go on pretending forever that we do know that vast American society, but deep inside we all know that we know nothing about it … [The program was presented] by an Arab journalist. He told us that America is not just about politics. There is more to America. There is an amazing success story.[7]

The second program, *Inside Washington*, takes viewers behind the scenes of the political process in Washington with guests such as Supreme Court Justice Antonin Scalia, Alexander Haig, and Congressional Representatives Howard L. Berman (D-California), Ileana Ros-Lehtinen (R-Florida), Tom Lantos (D-California), and Peter Hoekstra (R-Michigan). By being an Arabic-language network based in the United States, we have the opportunity to produce the type of program that can build bridges across real and perceived cultural gaps.

Even though it has only been on the air for four years, Alhurra is making inroads on the Arab media scene. Surveys conducted by independent research companies such as ACNielsen indicates that Alhurra TV has an estimated weekly reach of approximately 23 million people.[8] Of course Al Jazeera and Al Arabiya generally lead the pack, but Alhurra is definitely in the media mix. As mentioned above, Arab audiences traditionally look to three or four sources of information to distill the bias and discern the truth about any news item. In the short time that Alhurra has been on the air, it is developing its niche as one of these reliable sources for credible, accurate, and balanced news and information. Alhurra may not be the first place viewers go to watch the news, but we are becoming a destination in the news mix. This is a significant achievement for a U.S.-financed news network, especially when anti-American sentiment in the region is at an all time high.

In fact, preliminary research in Iraq shows that the weekly audience for Alhurra is at least as large—and probably larger—than that of Al Jazeera.[9] This could be in part because of Alhurra's commitment of a second channel, Alhurra-Iraq, providing Iraqi citizens with daily newscasts and talk shows that deal specifically with the challenges facing modern-day Iraq.

As more and more countries sponsor Arabic-language channels broadcasting to the Middle East, an already crowded market becomes even more competitive. As the "American channel," with objective news and open discussion of topics that are taboo on other channels, Alhurra is carving out its place in the growing Middle Eastern media marketplace. We welcome the competition and believe we can contribute to the growth of a journalistic practice in the Middle East that eschews emotion in favor of accuracy, objectivity, and a respect for the viewers' ability to decide.

Notes

1.   Mamoun Fandy, (*Un)Civil War of Words: Media and Politics in the Arab World* (Praeger Security International, 2007), 143.

2.   Interviews managed by InterMedia in Morocco (June 2007) and in Iraq (November 2007).

3.   InterMedia, interviews in Jordan (August 2006), and InterMedia Alhurra program review (December 2006).

4,   InterMedia focus groups in Bahrain (October 2003), and interviews in Jordan (June 2007).

5.   Hugh Miles, *Al-Jazeera: the Inside Story of the Arab News Channel that is Challenging the West* (New York: Grove Press, 2005), 73.

6.   Khaled Al Chami, "Admiring Alhurra's Egyptian Elections Coverage: Their newscasts have become like family in the Egyptian news environment," *Al-Quds Al-Arabi,* Sept. 7, 2005.

7.   Hazem el Ameen, "The Story of Jeans in Arab Eyes," *Al-Hayat,* Feb. 8, 2006.

8.   Surveys managed by InterMedia. Surveys conducted in 2007 include Algeria, Egypt, Jordan, Kuwait, Lebanon, Morocco (urban only), Saudi Arabia, UAE (Abu Dhabi and Dubai only) and Iraq. Bahrain, Qatar, and Tunisia were surveyed in 2006. Syria (primarily urban) was surveyed in 2005. New surveys for Syria are expected to be available in the first half of 2008.

9.   The newest survey data from Iraq (managed by InterMedia, September 2007) indicates weekly audiences for Alhurra at 55.6 percent of adults vs. 52.6 percent for Al Jazeera. This difference is within the margin of error for the survey, so it is possible that the audiences for the two stations are equivalent.

PART 4
STRUCTURE AND RESOURCES

11. Facing the Facts—And What to Do

John H. Trattner

THE UNITED STATES is approaching one of those junctures where a change of political command and policy outlook in Washington seems likely. Whether or not that happens, however, U.S. government–funded international radio broadcasting as it currently operates needs significant reshaping as a part of broader changes in American public diplomacy. In that effort, it is more important than ever to re-state some abiding truths about basic elements of the U.S. broadcasting picture—external and internal structure, resources, and content—and to look candidly at how they now stand.

EXTERNAL STRUCTURE

U.S. broadcasting will be most effective if it has global reach to leaders and major populations, and if it provides service in widely spoken world languages— English, Arabic, French, Chinese, Spanish, Russian—as well as in languages spoken by other key audiences, including non-Arab Muslim populations.

Amid increasingly partisan politics at home and badly damaged American credibility abroad, critical components of U.S. radio broadcasting in the last seven years have taken big cuts in English and ten foreign language services. The Voice of America's worldwide English service—the main national language of the United States and the leading common language abroad for business, diplomacy, and the Internet—was reduced from twenty-four hours daily to fourteen. In addition, a number of shortwave and AM relay stations have been dropped.

Proposals made by the Broadcasting Board of Governors (BBG) for the FY 2008 federal budget would have essentially wiped out what remains of Voice of America (VOA) English radio broadcasts around the world. Further, the proposals would have abolished or reduced thirteen additional VOA languages, including Russian on radio, as well as eight languages at Radio Free Europe/Radio Liberty and Radio Free Asia.[1]

John H. Trattner is an independent writer, with nonprofit clients in the fields of education, the environment, and international affairs.

Fortunately, Congress mandated a reversal of most of the cuts. But there are indications the BBG may seek to reinstate some reductions—including abolishing VOA worldwide English on radio—in the FY 2009 budget. The cuts could take effect as early as next October, just weeks before the U.S. national election. Astonishingly, the BBG is still trying to eliminate most U.S. English-language radio, while China, Russia, Iran, France, and Al Jazeera are expanding their English radio, television, or Internet services. Those broadcasters recognize what the United States apparently chooses to ignore: that English is an official language in seventy-four countries and that more than a billion people—educated leaders and opinion makers among them—speak it. Broadcasting in English, including even VOA's diminished output, has a large, global, sophisticated audience. Why would America ever wish to forego such a supremely important market, especially one that communicates in its own principal language? And why would it wish to do so, given the current tense, dangerous state of international affairs?

The impetus behind virtually all the newly proposed cuts has been (1) the perceived need to focus significantly more resources on the Arab world, Iran, Pakistan, Afghanistan, and other Muslim regions, notably including entire new networks aimed specifically at those areas; (2) the need to invest in new broadcast technologies while discarding old relay stations; and (3) the notion that shortwave listening is dropping dramatically.

Today, no one could reasonably argue against concentrating more attention on Muslim audiences. But in the rest of the listening world, a number of unfriendly political or media environments continue to impede people's access to information and ideas from the outside. U.S. broadcasting should not so arbitrarily weaken its reach to millions of listeners in non-Muslim areas whose attention and loyalty it has worked hard to achieve.

Nor can there be any dispute about investing in the new technologies that broaden and deepen broadcasting's impact. But it makes little sense to slash major relay stations—and yield valuable frequencies that others are eager to use—on the theory that shortwave is going out of fashion. The fact is that new technology may give shortwave's reception quality a significant boost in coming years. As other broadcasters are doing, the United States should conserve its capacity to deliver shortwave and digital AM when that time comes.

As for the shortwave market itself, listeners are not abandoning these frequencies in the precipitous way that some observers have recently predicted. A British researcher recently estimated a one-week worldwide shortwave audience at 306 million. Of the 184 million who listen to the BBC World Service on the radio every week, more than 100 million continue to use shortwave.[2] In a European Broadcasting Union poll in 2007, very few respondents planned to reduce their shortwave hours; many more hoped to expand shortwave broadcasting in the next ten to fifteen years to take advantage of evolving digital shortwave technology.[3]

Voice of America services, including worldwide English, should return to their pre-2001 status, with VOA reaffirmed as the centerpiece of American overseas broadcasting. For decades, VOA has been the only official U.S. worldwide overseas broadcast network and the only U.S.–sponsored broadcaster that carries official commentary. It has an established, influential audience. Even with recent cutbacks, it reaches 115 million listeners and viewers around the world each week, plus millions of Internet readers in forty-five languages. It is far too valuable to suffer emasculation in the service of temporary needs, however urgent.

Likewise, RFE/RL and RFA—with daily news, analysis, and current affairs programming of high value to particular audiences—should be preserved. Radio Sawa should restore the primacy of news and information that characterized the former VOA Arabic service. Radio and TV Marti should continue for the time being, but their missions and programming should keep pace with developments in Cuba in the approach and arrival of the post-Castro era. (Good insights into this could doubtless be mined among the Cuban American community, now increasingly characterized by people born in the United States.)

INTERNAL STRUCTURE

U.S. broadcasting will be most effective if it is, and is seen to be, strongly shielded from political manipulation. Further, it should be overseen by an entity independent of the federal executive branch, whose members collectively provide broad public, private, and nonprofit sector experience in broadcast journalism, the media industry, diplomacy, business, education, and research.

It is crucial to distinguish criticism of broadcasting content or policy from manipulation. It is one thing for a member of Congress, say, to complain that broadcasting is not serving U.S. goals when it includes opposing viewpoints or material that is unflattering to the United States. It is quite another if broadcasts are actually altered, by that or other pressures, to categorically exclude such content, when inclusion could boost credibility and provide comparisons validating America's commitment to a free flow of information and ideas.

That appears to have occurred at Radio Marti, as reported in a December 2006 editorial by the Chicago *Tribune* about the International Broadcasting Bureau's review of content on Marti. The Bureau's study, the newspaper said, found Marti had shied away from broadcasting news "that reflects badly on the administration that sponsors the shows or the Cuban exiles who produce them."[4] An anti-Castro bias on Marti might be tolerable—after all, those who listen know why the station is on the air. But airing only positive content about the sponsors and producers at the station is not tolerable. It's manipulation.

Another example is the harsh criticism leveled by former BBG Chairman Kenneth Y. Tomlinson at Alhurra (a U.S.–funded TV station) not long ago about what he regarded as inappropriate news content focused on Hezbollah and Hamas. That, and ensuing Congressional inquiries, could not have helped Alhurra efforts to build confidence among Muslim listeners that the station is seeking balance and reliability.

None of this is new. Disputes over the approach to content on international U.S. stations, including news content, date back at least to the early Reagan years. They have bloomed most intensely when the country finds itself at serious odds with a perceived adversary or in actual hostilities. At such times, U.S. administrations rediscover international broadcasting's potential as a propaganda instrument and want to step up its use for that purpose. Yet they lay hands on it at their peril. Those who have fought over the years for the objectivity of U.S. broadcasting were and are absolutely correct. They rightly see that manipulation merely renders U.S. broadcasting indistinguishable from the broadcasting of U.S. adversaries. If that vital difference disappears, so does much of the trust of its audience.

Which brings us to the oversight of U.S. broadcasting and the BBG itself. Created by Congress in 1994 as a bipartisan entity whose nine members (no more than four from one political party) are appointed by the president, the BBG is responsible for all U.S. nonmilitary overseas broadcasting. It makes policy, secures and allocates resources from Congress, oversees broadcast content, and conducts research.

Criticism of the BBG and its operations, much of it without regard to politics or ideology, appears to exceed praise. Typical is a comment by Mark Helmke, a senior Republican staffer of the Senate Foreign Relations Committee. As he puts it in an essay elsewhere in this anthology, "Through a curious provision in the 1994 act creating the Board, members can continue to serve after their terms have expired. This approach has become a political recipe for failure."[5] Helmke made that statement at a public forum in November 2006, when the terms of six BBG members had already expired.

In its 2006 annual report, the Broadcasting Board of Governors, describing its structure and mission, says in part that the board "in accordance with its enabling legislation … reviews and evaluates the effectiveness of the broadcast language service, and safeguards journalistic integrity." It continues, "This last function is of key importance to the board which sees as vital its role as a 'firewall' between BBG journalists and those who would seek to influence news coverage."

Moreover, the Broadcasting Act of 1994, reaffirmed in 1998 (Section 305), says that the Board, in carrying out its functions, "shall respect the professional independence and integrity of … its broadcasting services and grantees."

> Those who have fought over the years for the objectivity of U.S. broadcasting were and are absolutely correct. They rightly see that manipulation merely renders U.S. broadcasting indistinguishable to listeners from the broadcasting of U.S. adversaries.

The BBG, then, is supposed to act as a barrier against political interference with what its stations broadcast. But, as shown above, there is evidence suggesting that the BBG does not always honor in spirit this safeguarding function assigned it by law. The balance and credibility of U.S. broadcasting, and the trust of its audiences, are at risk. The firewall is not working as well as it should.

No attempt to insulate the governance and operations of U.S. broadcasting from manipulative pressures can succeed completely. Even if it were placed outside government altogether, immunity would not be absolutely airtight, and such a move would raise knotty questions of finance, mission, and relationship to government. In any case, moreover, government should have the right to communicate its views and preferences to the broadcast entity, wherever it is located, in a noncompulsory context.

There are two alternatives to consider here. Both would recast the accountability and reporting responsibilities of those who oversee U.S. broadcasting and remove the secretary of state from their midst. The first alternative would locate accountability and reporting functions in the Congress. The second would lodge accountability equally in the executive and legislative branches. In either case, accountability would in principle more closely resemble that found in such existing laws or institutions as the Inspector General Act of 1978, the National Endowment for Democracy, and the U.S. Institute of Peace. Either alternative would strengthen the bipartisan stature of oversight. Two other changes of language and tone also seem useful. One would drop the BBG title in favor of a less awkward, more illuminating designation (for example, the "agency for global broadcasting"). The other would reword the mission of U.S. broadcasting, as now stated by BBG, to read: "promote and sustain *self-government, human rights, and free expression and communication*" (replacing "freedom and democracy").

RESOURCES

U.S. broadcasting will be most effective if its funders recognize the imperative of adequate, stable, rationally distributed financial resources that constantly reflect technological advance and changing needs.

The FY 2008 and 2009 budget proposals continue on a track already littered with cutbacks in broadcasting services and transmitting capacity at VOA, Radio Free Europe/Radio Liberty, and Radio Free Asia since 2001. Whether these turn out to have been valid long-term decisions remains to be seen.

Either way, however, they are short-sighted. For one thing, no one knows where or who the most important broadcast audiences of the future will be. For another, it is easier to reduce or eliminate capacity than it is to restore or rebuild it. Doing so takes time and imposes costs that would not otherwise have been necessary. In the process, listeners drop away and staff skills and talent grow rusty or are lost.

A more logical, less expensive approach to funding would entail strategic, not tactical, decisions. It would recognize that adequate funding of international broadcasting (and public diplomacy as a whole) has become a long-term imperative; that it should respond to real and changing circumstances on the ground; and that it should be reasonably immune to budgetary expediency. Beginning with FY 2009, the annual appropriation for international broadcasting should be at least $712 million, which would include the restoration of all core services. The minimum operational benchmark at VOA should be set at 60 percent for maintenance and the multimedia enrichment of core programs, with the annual outlay for VOA not lower than $200 million, adjusted for inflation.

CONTENT

U.S. broadcasting will be most effective if it emphasizes hard news, adding other material including commentary and entertainment in differing mixes appropriate to the audiences and broadcast service in question. It should assert the positives about the United States, but also acknowledge the negatives and make room, where appropriate, for the views of others, including adversaries.

In some important respects U.S. broadcasting does not succeed in this regard. Where Muslim audiences are concerned, for instance, the BBG made a tactical decision that not only skewed the reach of its broadcasting but seemed to go against common sense. That was its commitment to build mass listenership, with reduced emphasis on reaching influential current and future elites. The board clearly misjudged with its quantity-over-quality decision to reduce news and information content in order to attract a larger Arab-speaking audience. The move eliminated VOA's full service Arabic program in favor of Radio Sawa, focused on pop music, entertainment, and young people. It's an approach that may have echoed the recipe concocted so successfully by Willis Conover years ago. But Conover's airtime was only a small proportion of VOA programming; by contrast, the predominance of entertainment and pop music heard on today's Radio Sawa seems counter to the national interest if the goal is to reach the listeners who matter the most.

Data from polls and anecdotal evidence indicate that Radio Sawa has a high percentage of young listeners but also that most of them tune in only for the entertainment. More people can hear Radio Sawa today than could hear VOA's former Arabic service but, before that service was eliminated, VOA was planning a major expansion of its broadcasting on the medium wave and FM frequencies where most people now hear Radio Sawa. It is thus arguable that Radio Sawa has a bigger audience, mainly for its entertainment content, but fewer desirable listeners than VOA Arabic had (and would have today) for its format of news and facts.

Certainly, U.S. international broadcasting should never ignore young people or mass audiences. Why, though, should it use big chunks of precious resources trying to fully compete for pop culture listeners with the Internet and a flood of other stations and communication platforms unknown in Conover's day? Instead, it should return to its former mission—to an emphasis on reaching leaders with news and information—and leave most of the entertainment to others.

• • •

Broadcasting is the one element of American public diplomacy that can reach millions of people more effectively than any other. In this of all eras, the United States cannot afford to steadily and irrationally prune the structure, withhold the crucial resources, or undermine the credibility that has earned it durable overseas broadcast audiences. That fact should be fundamental in debating the structure and resource levels that support U.S. broadcasting.

Notes

1. The proposals do include plans to strengthen VOA English on the Internet.
2. Graham Mytton, email correspondence to Alan Heil, July 23, 2007.
3. "Survey of Future HF Spectrum Requirements," European Broadcasting Union, Geneva, 2007.
4. "Sorry, Marti, Nobody's Listening," editorial, Chicago *Tribune*, Dec. 23, 2006, 20.
5. See Mark Helmke, chapter 12.

12. THE FUTURE OF U.S. INTERNATIONAL BROADCASTING

Mark Helmke

THE INTERNATIONAL BROADCASTING services, paid for by the U.S. government, face strategic and structural difficulties. At the structural level, the makeup of the Broadcasting Board of Governors (BBG), designed by Congress to attempt to ensure that the so-called political firewall remains strong, has turned the BBG into what from 2005 until a new chairman took office last June was a den of bickering partisan interests and conflicts.

Currently, two board seats are unfilled; and except for the membership on the board by the secretary of state, the terms of the other six board members have all expired. Through a curious provision in the 1994 law creating the board, members can continue to serve after their terms have expired. This approach has become a political recipe for failure. It proves that this plan to govern U.S. international broadcasting has failed. It's time to scrap the whole idea of the board, and reorganize.

The other structural problem is the crazy quilt combination of federal and nongovernment entities. Most members of Congress and their staffs, when first encountering the BBG organization chart, scratch their heads in disbelief and move on to issues that make more sense.

The strategic problems are more important. The structural problems hobbling international broadcasting are confounded by its lack of overall strategic direction within the national security and diplomatic apparatus of the federal government.

There is no consensus among the various agencies of the federal government, let alone Congress and the public, about what kind of war America is fighting and what are the best strategy and tactics to employ. There is a political consensus to rethink Iraq at both a strategic and tactical level, but beyond that, the political decision making process is adrift. There is a general recognition that strategic communications and public diplomacy

Mark Helmke is a long-time aide to U.S. Senate Foreign Relations Committee Chairman Richard G. Lugar.

are needed, but there is no agreement on who should conduct it, how it should be done, where it's needed, and at whom it should be directed.

The Pentagon has grown frustrated with the lack of direction and action from the State Department, and has decided to dismiss the work of BBG. By virtue of its vast financial resources, the Pentagon is taking over. I have seen no evidence that the Pentagon takes seriously anything that the international broadcasting entities do as contributing to American national security.

In July 2007, the Government Accountability Office (GAO) released a report to Senator Lugar on the evolving strategic communications and public diplomacy initiatives at the Departments of State and Defense, and the BBG. Since the GAO began this review at Senator Lugar's request in 2006, the Strategic Communications and Public Diplomacy Policy Coordinating Committee led by then-Undersecretary of State Karen Hughes began work, and a new national strategy for public diplomacy and strategic communications was released in June 2007.[1]

Previous GAO reports in 2003 and 2006, and the Defense Science Board Strategic Communications report in 2004, focused in part on the need for the State Department to take the lead on strategic communications and public diplomacy and adopt a "campaign-style" approach.

Every successful political and corporate communications campaign adopts such strategies and tactics, using polling and research to test messages and influence key audiences. As Senator Lugar says, "America has people who know how to do this." Yet, when it comes to the government, we continue to struggle and evolve, especially since the breakup of the U.S. Information Agency. The new State Department strategic communications plan recommends the "ABCDE" (audience, behavior, content, design, and evaluation) approach, which is Public Relations 101. It's a start.

The Pentagon, as the GAO report points out, is a lot more focused on the importance of strategic communications. Congress has given the Pentagon much more resources than it has given the State Department. This is a concern to Senator Lugar, just as is the Pentagon's growing role in foreign assistance.

In the GAO report, an unnamed BBG official is quoted as claiming that the Board is outside of strategic communications. This contention and the continuing debate over the role of U.S. government international broadcasting needs to be rejoined, especially in light of the GAO report on how the BBC coordinates with the Foreign Office.

Whither international broadcast is a moot point. It appears as uncertain as ever. Nevertheless, I work for a Senator who is perpetually optimistic, despite all the challenges he faces in arms control, democracy promotion, and energy security. So I offer a modest proposal, some of which I first made a few years ago at the Heritage Foundation.

During the last few months of the Bush administration, the White House, the State Department, and the Pentagon should attempt to lead a bipartisan effort to reorganize and reform America's strategic communications and public diplomacy operations.

The Smith-Mundt restrictions on communicating to American audiences have created an inherent conflict in American public diplomacy, and a political and bureaucratic contradiction. American public diplomacy is handicapped by these conflicts and contradictions. If Congress sees American public diplomacy as propaganda not fit for Americans, how is the rest of the world expected to view and understand it? The Smith-Mundt restrictions should be repealed. Let the public decide. Let the world see and hear America's open and democratic discussion.

Based on my understanding of the history, the United States government has had three different missions regarding international broadcasting.

The first is to use broadcasting and other communications techniques to help explain and promote American foreign policy: America's commitment to democracy, human rights, and economic opportunity, and—this is the hardest part—the diversity, complexity and inherent messiness of American political decision making.

The second mission is to support indigenous media reporting on democracy, human rights, and transparency in countries that do not have a free press.

The third mission builds on the second, and that is to support the development of free, fair, and self-sustaining free press in those same countries.

Presently, the international broadcasting entities embrace all three missions. This is counterproductive. This first mission is public diplomacy. The second and third involve fostering international democratic institutions. These missions are complementary, but need to be separated.

The first mission of promoting and explaining American foreign policy is what the VOA has long been about. This the VOA should continue, and it should expand its work to involve Congress by serving, in part, as an international C-SPAN.

Colleagues of mine traveled around the world in the fall of 2006 surveying the work of American embassies. The November mid-term elections that year were of great interest to almost all of the foreign nationals they encountered. This nuance in American foreign policy is an important point. Presidents are not absolute dictators of American foreign policy. How effectively does American international broadcasting communicate the complexity of the American decision-making process? I'm not convinced we do. How sophisticated are VOA, Radio Free Europe/Radio Liberty, and Alhurra reporters in covering the deliberations of the Senate Foreign Relations Committee? Deficient, based on my thirty years of experience.

> **If Congress sees American public diplomacy as propaganda not fit for Americans, how is the rest of the world expected to view and understand it?**

To advance and improve VOA, no independent bipartisan commission is needed. Voice of America belongs in the State Department, monitored in a bipartisan way through the Constitutional oversight powers of the Senate Foreign Relations Committee, and House Foreign Affairs Committee.

The second mission of international broadcasting has been supporting indigenous media reporting in countries without a free press. This has long been the work of Radio Free Europe/Radio Liberty, and recently Radio Free Asia and Radio and TV Marti. They should become truly independent nonprofits, run by independent boards, and financed by Congress. Their jobs are to put themselves out of business over the long-term. In doing so, they should coordinate their efforts with the National Endowment for Democracy, which Congress and Secretary Rice have now designated as the strategic coordinator for the development of free, fair, and viable free press.

If we review the BBG's various entities in this light, questions arise about Alhurra and Radio Sawa. If the goal is to develop free and independent media in the Arab-speaking world, then they too should have an independent board and receive Congressional funding based on a plan to eventually get off the government dime. If the goal of Alhurra and Radio Sawa is to serve as a platform for explaining and promoting American foreign policy, they should be merged back into VOA.

Since 9/11, too much of the public diplomacy debate has been about tactics—buy advertisements, start a new TV station—and not about strategy. We need to reach a consensus on public diplomacy strategies before we get bogged down and waste more money on tactics that may or may not work.

Notes

1. GAO, *U.S. Public Diplomacy: Actions Needed to Improve Strategic Use and Coordination of Research*, GAO-07-904, (Washington, DC: GAO), 2007.

13. ROUNDTABLE: VETERAN U.S. DIPLOMATS AND INTERNATIONAL BROADCASTERS WALTER R. ROBERTS AND BARRY ZORTHIAN

October 2007

Moderator: Alan L. Heil Jr.

HEIL: As we look ahead to a new century of new challenges, what do you see as the mission—or perhaps there are several missions—of U.S. international broadcasting?

ROBERTS: U.S. international broadcasting is a vital part of public diplomacy. Indeed, it is one of the most important aspects of public diplomacy because there is no other medium at the disposal of the public diplomat that reaches as many people in one fell swoop as international broadcasting. In addition to the global Voice of America (VOA), other broadcasting networks, by some called surrogate stations, were created by the U.S. government over the years. The term "surrogate" was first used when Radio Free Europe (RFE) was founded in 1950. It was explained then that nongovernmental organizations and personalities outside communist Eastern Europe created broadcasting stations that would act as if they were located within a free Eastern Europe. There was supposedly no connection with any government, including ours. As you know that secret became a non-secret in the late 1960s, and RFE's connection with the U.S. government was revealed. But our relations with the communist governments of Eastern Europe were so dicey at that time that the U.S. government allowed these broadcasts to continue on an openly appropriated basis.

Walter R. Roberts joined the Voice of America in 1942 and served in public diplomacy posts in Washington and overseas, including as associate director of the U.S. Information Agency and as a memeber of the U.S. Advisory Commission on Public Diplomacy.

Barry Zorthian is a former vice president of Time, Inc., and a retired senior Foreign Service officer with tours in India and Vietnam. He spent thirteen years with the Voice of America, the last five as program manager, and served on the Board of Radio Free Europe/Radio Liberty by appointment of George H. W. Bush.

HEIL: Barry, how do you see it?

ZORTHIAN: Well, look, this is a new century of new challenges: the projection, the communication by all kinds of elements in this communications-information world. I think there's a critical role still for U.S. international broadcasting that supports, adds to, provides understanding, if you will, of the United States and particularly the U.S. position on critical international issues. So the role remains the same. There is a mission of communicating the United States, in all its forms, all its aspects, all its warts, if you will, all its policies. And that continues even though the information stage is so very crowded today.

HEIL: Walter, you've had close exposure in your career to both the Voice of America and the surrogate broadcasters. How would you organize, rationalize, this galaxy of overseas networks?

ROBERTS: You ask how I would organize, rationalize this galaxy of overseas networks. Alan, I can't. No other country has such a mish-mash of broadcasters (VOA, Radio Free Europe/Radio Liberty, Radio Free Asia, Cuba Broadcasting, Radio Farda, Radio Sawa, Alhurra). All of these stations could be run by VOA. They are not surrogate stations, as I understand the term. If real surrogate broadcasts are still needed for certain areas, in my view, they should be undertaken on a covert basis by military or intelligence agencies.

HEIL: This, as you say, is a new communications age. How would you, as veteran executives of U.S. international broadcasting, adjust to the variegated audience needs and media environments that Walter just described?

ROBERTS: The information revolution has indeed created a different media environment; whereas sixty-five years ago, international broadcasting was confined to shortwave transmissions, there are several other means now available to reach the listener, indeed the viewer and reader, when you think of television and the Internet.

ZORTHIAN: Let me add that, over a period of time, international broadcasting, projected as effectively as possible, is still only one element of this nation's communication with other peoples. Walter is absolutely right: it is a critical part of "public diplomacy" but also almost separate from it. But there are many other elements communicating on behalf of the United States, or, if you will, with the United States as a source: American corporations overseas, American media going on the air, NGOs and so on. There are cultural and educational exchanges funded by the government. All are part of this nation's communications overseas. International broadcasting is one element in that. It has a particular job, a particular role of projecting America, its government, its people, its values, its nature, its role in the world in an objective non-partisan manner, and that is what it has to provide.

HEIL: Can the nongovernmental organizations and the government-funded networks be somehow brought together or coordinate their efforts better as we look ahead to the new century?

ROBERTS: Yes, indeed. I have studied the international broadcasting operations of various countries and it seems to me that the British system functions very well. I realize that the BBC not only has an external service but also, of course, a domestic operation. When VOA was created in 1942, no non-commercial domestic radio operations existed in the United States. So VOA was established as a government department. But today there is the Corporation for Public Broadcasting, there is National Public Radio, NPR. The landscape has changed radically.

To turn VOA from a government department to a grantee agency would solve the perennial question as to whether a government employee can be an objective journalist. Of course, he or she can be, as years of credible broadcasting by VOA has demonstrated. But the question pops up again and again.

HEIL: Barry, is that your take on it? Can you be journalistically independent if you are a government entity?

ZORTHIAN: I underline that there's no set answer to the question. The BBC model of a semi-private organization is a perfectly valid one. Other structures can operate. What if you put broadcasting into the Corporation for Public Broadcasting in the United States? Or in the State Department? Or under an agency that would be a revival of the U.S. Information Agency? What you can't do is to insist that a government agency exercise unchecked control of the product of the outfit. To make that product legitimate, that agency has to be under the management, direction, and execution of people who do not have a particular axe to grind, who are responsible non-partisan observers and communicators. You know, there are various options here. All of them can work, if you have the right people and their concepts, ideas, and professionalism apply.

HEIL: Now we have the question always, of limited resources.   Newton Minow a few years ago said there ought be a standard appropriation for U.S. public diplomacy generally, and U.S. broadcasting particularly. The standard would be the equivalent of 1 percent of expenditures of the U.S. Defense Department about equally divided in a separate appropriation between broadcasting and public diplomacy activities such as cultural exchanges. Is that a fair allocation, given the demands of new technologies?

> Looking at public diplomacy budgets of other countries, comparatively, the U.S. budget is small. Determining its adequate size should be left to foreign affairs, public diplomacy, and communications specialists, and not, as it has been done for years, to the Office of Management and Budget.
>
> —Roberts

ROBERTS: I do not think we should deal with percentages of the Defense Department. We should establish an independent task force that should come up with an ideal but realistic budget for public diplomacy in general and international broadcasting in particular. Looking at public diplomacy budgets of other countries, comparatively, the U.S. budget is small. Determining its adequate size should be left to foreign affairs, public diplomacy, and communications specialists, and not, as it has been done for years, to the Office of Management and Budget.

HEIL: Resources, Barry?

ZORTHIAN: Alan, I'm probably in a minority on this. Frankly, it's a tempting thought that Newt Minow has put out: 1 percent of a Defense Department budget of $500 billion, give or take a few billion. This is $5 billion. I don't know what the public diplomacy area would do with $5 billion, nearly four times its present budget. I don't think it needs it. Maybe it needs an expensive hardware expansion in broadcast transmission and the various means of communication. Is the $600 million today for broadcasting enough? My instinct is to say yes, if it is properly spent. Is it being properly spent? I have questions. Do we need to put all the millions we're putting into Alhurra, are there more effective ways of doing it? So unlimited expansion with billions floating around is something I would question. Maybe the whole operation would grow up to it, to where it needs it for technical innovation, higher quality programming, and so on. But I sure would not try to solve the problem as we do in so many other areas, by just throwing money at it. We need some basic concepts, efficient operations, straightening them all out, and a real focus on what our missions are, and the execution of these.

HEIL: Basic concepts … efficient operations … straightening them out all seem to be related to structure. What is the best structure, or division of labor, for U.S. international broadcasting in 2009 and beyond?

> **Is the $600 million today for broadcasting enough? My instinct is to say "yes," if it is properly spent. Is it being properly spent? I have questions.**
>
> **—Zorthian**

ZORTHIAN: If we were starting off fresh and could establish whatever might make sense, I would advocate a concept of VOA broadcasting in what I would call world languages—English, Russian, Arabic, Spanish, Mandarin, Swahili, perhaps French, and maybe a South Asian Hindi—and consider broadcasting to smaller—not lesser—countries on a case-by-case basis. Can we reach the audience we want best on the Internet or by local placement? Does the target audience need surrogate broadcasting because of internal restrictions on the media? The audience the Voice of America should want to reach in this age of what Joseph Nye calls "the paradox of plenty, informationally" can be reached best through these world languages, and additionally by a careful analysis of a number of the smaller countries. It may be difficult to get this kind of pattern because of domestic ethnic political pressures, but it is a goal I suggest makes sense.

That said, I'm not sure there is an ideal structure for VOA absent a completely independent organization under a properly selected and mandated Board of Governors that is committed to the VOA charter and is financed by the government. Are the National Endowments for the Arts or Humanities or the National Academy of Science possible precedents? Day-to-day administration should be provided by a CEO of unquestioned professional credentials, retained on a multi-year contract to shield him or her from political pressure. The governing board should provide only general oversight, but zealously protect the journalistic integrity of the Voice.

While the State Department should not manage the VOA, it certainly should be a primary source in the determination of language broadcast priorities and provision of background information on foreign policies and actions. On the other hand, surrogate, or tactical broadcast networks, do not project the United States, but play the role of independent media where none exist in tightly controlled societies. They project the interests and viewpoints of a potentially free people. It is certainly justified to have both VOA and surrogate networks broadcasting in the same language to the same country. We had VOA and RFE/RL for more than forty years during the Cold War and the two, with distinctly different missions, reinforced each other in the former Soviet Union and Eastern Europe and were well worth the cost.

ROBERTS: Historically, VOA graduated from language broadcasts—originally English, German, French and Italian—to country broadcasts. At first, the language broadcasts were practically identical in content, but over time the broadcasts were adapted to the target audience. They were VOA and not surrogate broadcasts. As I said before, in my opinion, the best structure would be the Voice of America as the sole U.S. international broadcaster. VOA would be responsible to a board. Barry has persuasively outlined the structure and responsibilities of such a board. I consider it vital that VOA restore a twenty-four hour English service. All necessary transmitters should be taken out of mothballs. VOA should also broadcast in such foreign languages as recommended by the foreign policy establishment of the United States in general, and the public diplomacy directorate in particular.

ZORTHIAN: I agree with Walter that it is essential that the core language in any broadcast structure be English, our national language and the language used by an estimated 700 million people around the world. I question strongly the merits of reported efforts by the Broadcasting Board of Governors to severely reduce our English broadcasts in order to pay for a continuing expansion of Middle East language services such as Radio Sawa and Alhurra television in Arabic. If English were cut this year or next, there would be no broadcast of any kind under the label of the official Voice of America to the Middle East, from the borders of Iran all the way to Morocco. No English, and no Arabic. Similarly, the Board's closure of many shortwave relay stations over the past five years has been extremely shortsighted. Shortwave still commands huge audiences outside of North America. The retrieval of shortwave frequencies given up by the United States, requires an immediate and determined rescue effort. Digital shortwave is one of the new technologies that may gain listeners long term, and we should be ready for that eventuality.

HEIL: Whatever the structure and technological challenges—and there are many options—how do you balance audience needs and U.S. interests? How do you assure the journalistic integrity and credibility if broadcasting, as Congress and the Executive Branch often suggest, is the conveyor of an official message? Walter?

ROBERTS: The objective of public diplomacy is to create a climate overseas that is favorable to the United States. It goes way beyond official messages. It includes information about American society, culture, history, and many other special features commonly known as Americana. The Voice America has for many years conveyed these messages in a journalistic framework and still does so today.

ZORTHIAN: There are a number of aspects of this, Alan. They all got distilled through the blood, sweat, and tears of the 1950s and 1960s that led, under President Gerald Ford, to the legal endorsement of the VOA charter. And the VOA charter tried to face up to this problem: the presentation of actions by this government, by this society, in a responsible manner … a discussion of those, a projection, if you will, of U.S. government policies and their execution. Professionals do that skillfully. They don't do it in a ham-handed, lecturing fashion. They do an honest, straightforward projection of those policies that also meets the requirements of journalistic integrity. There's no reason you can't project U.S. policy in ways that reflect both the criteria of professional journalism and your mission. Rather than an "official" U.S. government editorial that raises questions about the independence of the Voice of America, the use of a "diplomatic correspondent" who analyzes U.S. policy and policy debates is one way of handling it. There are others. The credibility of the VOA, which took years—even decades—to establish was built on that principle. It was not an abandonment of its mission of conveying an official message. It was a presentation of that message in a responsible, balanced, accurate way. That is in the interest of the United States government.

HEIL: Finally, as seasoned observers of the evolution of U.S. international broadcasting in the last century, what briefly would you counsel for this activity and those who will lead it in the century ahead?

ZORTHIAN: A number of steps have to be taken. One, the technical means of program delivery have to be developed. Walter and I are regarded as two old-timers who want to re-live the past. That's not the case. Yes, modern communication has to be utilized, and that may mean development of new technical capabilities, whether that be the Internet, AM and FM radio, television, and so on. And that may take some money and resources, despite what I said earlier. Resources should be provided for that. Two, the staff for these operations has to be developed, I think, on a non-partisan, non-ideological, non-political basis: professionals in state of the art media projecting an accurate projection of the United States in a responsible manner, both the pros and the cons. Three, there should be coordination under management that provides oversight but does not try to alter for domestic political reasons the missions of these organizations and their efforts. Those missions have to be established, enforced and directed by professionals who have a real feel for their responsibilities.

ROBERTS: I agree that the big change is in the area of technology. VOA broadcasts will continue to be guided by the VOA charter that is as applicable today as it was when it was adopted in 1976. Of course, the VOA broadcast format has evolved just as domestically, for instance, the CBS Evening News today has a different shape than when Douglas Edwards started it in 1948. When VOA began, all we had was shortwave broadcasting. Now we have the Internet and, of course, television. So it is the new technical means of conveying our message that have changed. But the basic mission of communicating with the people of the world directly by radio has not changed.

PART 5
NEW MEDIA

14. New Technology and the Future of International Broadcasting

Nicholas J. Cull

As the digital revolution sweeps the globe, international broadcasting is trying to keep up. A practice that was once a monopoly of a familiar line-up of state-funded broadcasters and a handful of faith-based stations is now open to a wide range of competitors. Challengers range from full-scale commercial international news and entertainment stations to single individuals whose blogs, podcasts, and other user-generated content is available to a global audience, should anyone care to seek it out. One response to this challenge is merely to recite a catalogue of new gadgets that the well-equipped broadcaster should embrace to function in the digital world, but this is to miss the point of the fundamental shifts taking place in the relationship between the audience and the broadcaster, and the full implications of that shift for the process of public diplomacy.

Theoretical Foundations

Before contemplating the interface of new technology and international broadcasting for public diplomacy, it will help to clarify terminology. The immediate issue here is that these terms are by no means universally accepted. A substantial portion of the state-funded international broadcasting community maintains that its work is not "public diplomacy."[1] The claim is based on a misunderstanding of the extent to which the practice of public diplomacy is linked to advocacy. A simple definition of public diplomacy holds that it is an international actor's attempt to accomplish the ends of foreign policy by engaging with a foreign public. If the policy intent is there, and the public audience is there, then the activity is public diplomacy regardless of the nature of any information exchanged.

Nicholas J. Cull is professor of public diplomacy at the University of Southern California, where he directs the master's program in public diplomacy.

There are five key ways in which this engagement can take place:

(1) listening—the collection of information and opinion from a foreign public for the purposes of better policy formation;

(2) advocacy—the transmittal of information angled to promote a particular policy;

(3) cultural diplomacy—outreach using culturally based techniques such as language education or artistic performance, usually with a long term or fairly loose political agenda;

(4) exchange diplomacy—engagement through the mutual exchange of persons; and

(5) international broadcasting—engagement using radio, television, or Internet to reach a foreign public.

THE DISTINCTIVENESS OF INTERNATIONAL BROADCASTING

While international broadcasting can overlap with the other forms of public diplomacy, it is set apart by two major factors.[2] The first is the technical nature of its task, which requires an infrastructure wholly different from that of the other forms. The second is the ethical foundation of international broadcasting and its core component: news. For advocacy to succeed, it needs to be not only plausible but close enough to the source of foreign policy to be relevant. For international broadcasting to succeed, it needs a reputation for credibility that is undermined by proximity to the source of foreign policy. It needs a track record of balance and a willingness to present the bad news as well as the good. Hence, broadcasting is a component of public diplomacy that necessarily diverges in operating practices from the best known component: advocacy.

One problem for any international broadcaster is that, like any bureaucracy, it tends to develop an institutional purpose to perpetuate itself rather than to discharge the function for which it was designed or which it has come to fulfill in the broader system. The function of international broadcasting is to serve the ends of the funding-actor's foreign policy by creating and disseminating content devised within confines of the ethical framework of news accepted by that actor.[3] It should not be wedded to any one method of creation or dissemination, such as shortwave radio or FM affiliate broadcasting. Rather, it should define itself around its content: multilingual news provision.

THE PROBLEM OF CONTENT

There are two core concepts for the content of international broadcasting. These may be caricatured as "all about me" and "all about you." In the

United States, these concepts were each served by separate broadcasters with a distinct mission. The Voice of America's charter mandated not only news but also the presentation to the world of "American life and thought," and government policy and debates on the policies. Surrogate broadcasters such as Radio Free Europe and Radio Liberty (RFE/RL) were set to provide a substitute for dysfunctional local media in target areas. In reality, international broadcasters have always blended these ingredients according to the needs of their audiences and demands of their funders. Most non-American broadcasters mix surrogate and informational/cultural content in their output without ill effect, suggesting perhaps that the ancient dispute between VOA and RFE/RL owes more to local competition for limited resources than universal principles.

INTERNATIONAL BROADCASTING AND NEW TECHNOLOGY

The basic approach to new technology is to use it as a substitute for existing services. When an international broadcast's language service is directed toward a country with good Internet connectivity, it makes sense to switch to that service from shortwave, which is notoriously expensive to transmit and awkward to receive, to an online stream. Internet-only services now abound across the BBC, RFE/RL, VOA, and other broadcasters. New technology also has the potential to provide collateral services such as news feeds and program archives.

VOA began this sort of activity in the mid-1990s. Today, VOA stories are easy to locate, and they pop up unbidden along side those of Reuters and other agencies on Google News and other platforms. But this is just the tip of the iceberg. VOA and RFE/RL now have their own RSS feed. VOA also transmits audio news feeds in English and ten other languages for Internet-enabled phones and data devices.[4] A daily VOA email service is available, offering an English world news summary, an African news summary, or news for Zimbabwe.[5] VOA has begun trial podcasts of a daily selection of key programs including *Special English News*, *Press Conference USA*, *Reporter's Notebook*, and *Our World*.[6] Since the summer of 2007, VOA's weekday phone-in English show *Talk to America*, launched in 1995, has been replaced by a weekly Web-chat version branded T2A. Guests have included a wide range of authors, an astronaut, the president's daughter, an immigration attorney, and a smattering of VOA's home grown talent, including correspondent Al Pessin and Ken Berman, the Director of Internet Technology at VOA's parent International Broadcasting Bureau, who appeared on November 7, 2007, to discuss Circumventor, software developed in part with VOA funding to help listeners in China and other locations subject to Internet blocking to access the medium freely.[7]

THE WAY AHEAD: THE MESSAGE IN THE MEDIUM

While this work is admirable, it could be seen as "putting old wine in new bottles." The essential product has not changed, yet new media operate very differently from the old. Whereas the old analogue media were vertical, characterized by a mighty central provider sending material down and out to listeners around the world, in the new media environment messages are increasingly passed horizontally. Moreover, given that materials can pass as easily in any direction across the network, for the first time a broadcaster can receive information as easily as it can transmit it.

> The essential product has not changed, yet new media operate very differently from the old. Whereas the old analogue media were vertical, characterized by a mighty central provider sending material down and out to listeners around the world, in the new media environment messages are increasingly passed horizontally.

The potential for interactive programming goes far beyond a carefully screened phone-in or weekly Web chat. The *BBC World Service* has led the way with a new generation of interactive international broadcasting shows like *Africa Have Your Say*, in which the audience not only participates in a dialogue but proposes issues for future discussion. This program, which airs three mid-day hours a week, has become a major site for African self expression, with questions and comments coming in through direct calls, emails, and text messages. Programs generated by audience feedback include treatments of taboo subjects like suicide, as well as the expected developmental agenda subjects like corruption and community relations.[8] There is an obvious need to explore further ways to develop greater audience involvement and make better use of user-generated content. In so doing, the broadcaster will be deploying a source that some research (including the annual Edelman Trust Barometer survey) indicates has unparalleled credibility among audiences; that is, "people like me."[9]

RETHINKING THE MISSION

In order to prosper in the era of new media, the international broadcaster needs to develop a new sense of its own situation. As an international content generator, it must accept that its product may no longer reach the end user at the time of or even in the form of its original transmission. It is like a water utility which once piped a product from the reservoir through a filtration plant and out to a million faucets. It now has to accept that its product may be bottled by its user and passed on to a whole new audience.

One advantage which the best-known international broadcasters enjoy in this new world is the recognition and credibility of their brand. Messages crafted by VOA, RFE/RL, or the BBC stand an excellent chance of being relayed further along peer-to-peer networks because of their inherent credibility. As voices proliferate in cyberspace, the value of a strong and credible brand is enhanced rather than diminished. The established broadcasters are the Evian and Perrier in the marketplace. As international broadcasters shift to a system in which particular programs or even items within programs can be selected and transmitted by individual members of the audience, the task of the broadcaster is to make a range of material available within its ethical framework and to help the audience make its own selection. Every audience member who selects and passes information further along his or her peer-to-peer network operates as his or her own editor. They decide whether they want a surrogate service to depict their world, a voice to explain the United States, or, very likely, both. Attempts to link surrogate and advocacy or cultural content (for example, by embedding a VOA editorial in a regional news summary or a news broadcast in a music program) could detract from otherwise eminently shareable content and limit its share-ability.

Conversely, anything the content provider can do to promote the share-ability of its output—making content easy to post onto a blog or even easy to "mash" into a new user generated form—will improve its reach and engage a wide range of multipliers for its mission. One obvious way to take advantage of the credibility and creativity that rests in the audience is through competitions for user-generated content on a theme that serves a particular policy objective, trusting that the material created for this purpose will gain its own momentum and be circulated on peer-to-peer networks in exactly the same way as a joke, a rumor, or an urban legend.[10]

The connection of each person on the planet one to the other holds immense promise for democratization. Anything that a public diplomacy actor or international broadcaster can do to connect its target audience, including investment in wireless projects, creation of Internet-cafes, investment in workable real-time translation software, or assisting with the acquisition of basic English skills, will help. It should also be recognized that the broadcaster would do well to help maintain existing connections by supporting or lobbying for the appropriate international and domestic regulatory regimes.

WORDS OF CAUTION

While the potential of new technology is impressive, major broadcasters would be ill advised to withdraw completely from shortwave, medium-wave, or FM delivery. Key audiences around the world still rely on shortwave, and recent events in Burma have served as an object lesson in the need to retain a "surge capacity" in that band. Similarly, the speed with which Russia's President Putin and Pakistan's President Musharraf have been able to silence VOA FM affiliates in their territory also speaks powerfully to the wisdom of maintaining an option to use traditional technology.

Finally, the focus on objectives in international broadcasting should help refine the approach. If a particular service has a developmental objective, such as democratization, the broadcaster should take care that its service does not somehow stifle the evolution of indigenous voices in the target country. One way of linking international broadcasting and development goals is by developing a communication-related NGO under the brand of the broadcaster, as with the creation of the BBC World Service Trust in the UK.

CONCLUSION

In conclusion, new technology opens many more opportunities for international broadcasters than it closes, but getting the most from the future requires an openness to the special challenges of working in a peer-to-peer environment. The established mechanisms for prescribing the quality of an international broadcasting product—such as the Voice of America charter—remain essential as ever. The credibility of a broadcaster's brand will determine that broadcaster's reach and the ability of its messages to travel as far as possible along the rapidly expanding channels of the new network society.

Notes

1. This claim is routinely made by representatives of America's "surrogate broadcasters," who draw a distinction between their work and the "public diplomacy" mission of Voice of America. See, for example, *Understanding the Mission of U.S. International Broadcasting*, McCormick-Tribune Conference series, April 2007, online at www.hudson.org/files/pdf_upload/52693_McCormick.pdf.

2. Broadcasting overlaps with other forms of public diplomacy by several means; for example, *listening* through audience research; *advocacy* through its editorials; *cultural diplomacy* through music, arts, and language programming; and *exchange diplomacy* through exchanges of programming, facilities, or personnel.

3. Balanced news does not look the same on all stations that claim to present it.

4. The languages are Albanian, Chinese, Farsi, Indonesian, Korean, Turkish, Russian, Serbian, Spanish, and Vietnamese. Further services are imminent. www.voanews.com/english/mobile.cfm.

5. For details, see www.voanews.com/english/email-subscription.cfm.

6. For details, see www.voanews.com/english/podcasts.cfm.

7. For details of T2A, see www.voanews.com/english/t2a.cfm.

8. Author interview with Jerry Timmins, BBC World Service head of Africa and the Middle East, March 2007.

9. On the credibility of "people like me," see www.edelman.com/news/ShowOne.asp?ID=102.

10. This sort of material is known as a *meme*, and the creation of a meme in the age of the network society is equivalent to hitting the jackpot.

15. TRENDS IN NEW MEDIA

Mark Maybury

MEDIA, AND THE INFORMATION THEY CONVEY, can be a force multiplier or a force divider. Media have transformed from a classically centralized production and dissemination model to a model characterized by highly distributed production and personalized environments.

Key trends include the following:

- A shift from centralized to distributed production and broadcast
- The rise of citizen reporting
- An increase in interactive, online news reporting and services
- A significant reduction in audience sizes in traditional media (for example, an annual reduction of 2-3 percent in national newspaper circulation)
- An increase in heterogeneity; for example, magazines, newspapers, and Web sites focused at increasingly specific demographics
- An increase in the diversity of distribution platforms, often displacing traditional broadcast or subscription platforms
- Microtracking of advertising revenue in digital media
- A rise of mobile platforms
- Continued success of both subscription and advertising business models
- A rise of regional and/or socio-cultural focused broadcasters
- A proliferation of new technologies and information services

Dr. Mark Maybury is executive director of MITRE's Information Technology Division. He serves on the Air Force Scientific Advisory Board and the board of the Object Management Group and is a member of the steering committee for ACM IUI.

The author would like to thank Bob Lucky and Bruce Gregory for sharing ideas regarding the future of media, and he especially appreciates Bruce Gregory, Eric Hughes, and John Boiney for their comments on drafts.

These trends, fuelled by the overall digitization and proliferation of media, are transforming the media landscape, resulting in increased complexity and interdependency.

AUDIENCES

Globally, roughly 4 billion people have access to television, 2 billion have mobile phones, and 1 billion people are connected to the Internet, as illustrated in figure 1. With a half billion European mobile phones, nearly half of Europeans regularly watch TV on the Internet. The most popular activity on cell phones besides talking is the use of text/instant messaging,[1] with youths the primary user.[2]

South Korea, as perhaps the most connected country on the planet and often a harbinger of future trends, provides an interesting case in mobile television subscribers. While there are presently 6 million terrestrial-based mobile TV subscribers, Korea's SK Telecom reports 2 million satellite-based subscribers.[3] Since many of these mobile devices include video recorders and wi-fi Internet connectivity, the volume of information produced and the diversity of media conveying that information is increasing. The technology also lays the foundation to support a citizen reporter; and likewise for a citizen recorder, if not a citizen censor.

FIGURE 1. ACCESS TO MEDIA GLOBALLY (IN BILLIONS)

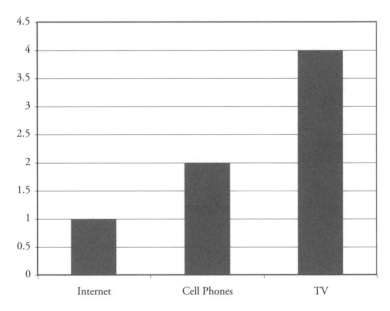

While Asia, Europe, and North America represent several hundred millions of Internet users each, North America, Australia, and Europe are the most developed markets, with about 70 percent, 54 percent, and 40 percent market penetration, respectively (see figure 2). Latin America, Asia, Middle East, and Africa all have 20 percent or less Internet penetration, with Africa the lowest at only 4 percent. Africa and the Middle East have a growth rate about three times the world average. With an average penetration of 18 percent of global population, more than 80 percent of the individuals on the planet are not yet reached by the Internet. Notably, global connectivity and dissemination of information and services means that adoption rates can be much faster than with traditional technologies. For example, in order to reach a market size of 50 million participants, it took thirty-eight years for radio, but only thirteen years for television. In contrast, the Internet made the 50 million person audience mark in only four years.[4]

In the United States, adults ages 25-49 currently spend only about thirty minutes a day reading books and magazines, about an hour a day listening to recorded music, and an hour using the Internet, but between four to five hours watching television.[5] A closer look at radio reveals some interesting trends, including a gradual erosion of traditional audiences for terrestrial radio and the rapid growth of Internet radio correlated with

FIGURE 2. INTERNET PENETRATION BY WORLD REGION (PERCENTAGE)

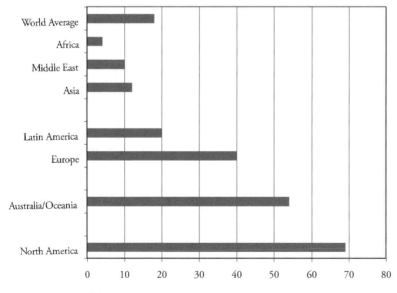

Source: internetworldstats.com, 2007.

wireless Internet penetration. XM and Sirius satellite radio presently represent, respectively, over 8 and 6.5 million subscribers in the United States alone, whereas podcasting represents just over 2 million users with a slower growth rate. While the current audience is only about a half million, high definition (HD) radio is projected to grow rapidly.[6]

GLOBAL, INTERACTIVE, PERSONALIZED: WIKIS AND BLOGS

Media continue to evolve, increasing global reach, personalization, and interactivity. The Internet has proliferated global reach of information services. For example, wikis and blogs are efficient and effective information creation and communication mechanisms. Wikipedia, the online encyclopedia Jimmy Wales created in 1999 and then named Nupedia, today attracts 4.8 million registered users, and 1,200 volunteers regularly edit over 2 million (English) articles. Impressively, there are only about ten full-time employees for this large information collection. Foreign language versions exist in over 100 languages for well over 5 million articles in 2007, although content is not always consistent across languages. In 2007, the Oxford English Dictionary recognized "wiki" as an English word. Quality of this user-authored and -edited encyclopedia has arisen as an issue. To ensure accuracy, verification, quality sourcing, and elimination of personal opinion, Wikipedia employs a series of consensus-based vetting processes ("wisdom of the crowds"). Stephen Colbert coined the term "wikiality," meaning "truth by consensus." Just as anyone can submit an article, also anyone can initiate an "Article for Deletion" (AfD) review process if they believe a contribution is substandard. In December 2005, forty-two comparative reviews of Wikipedia and Encyclopaedia Britannica online science articles found 123 errors in Encyclopaedia Britannica and 162 errors in Wikipedia (for averages of 2.9 and 3.9 errors per article, respectively.) Of these errors, eight were considered serious (for example, misinterpretations), four from each source.[7]

Blogs are interactive Web sites that allow any user to post information or comment on posted information. Blogs have exploded as focused, interactive, and often individualized Web sites for information sharing. Blogs have grown in size and diversity, supporting a wide range of communities of interest. To gain a sense of the magnitude of blogging, as of September 2007, there were over 100 million blogs with about one hundred thousand new blogs created daily. There are 1.3 million posts per day, or about 54K an hour. The top fifty blogs consist mostly of traditional media sites, such as New York Times, Yahoo! News, CNN, MSNBC. Language posts are about 40 percent English, 33 percent Japanese, 10 percent Chinese, 10 percent western European languages, 2 percent Russian, and 1 percent Farsi. The fact that Farsi has moved into the top ten languages of the blogosphere is indicative of escalating discussion of socio-political issues in the Middle East and diaspora.

Really Simple Syndication (RSS), and similar XML (eXtensible Markup Language) formats such as RDF Site Summary and Rich Site Summary, enable users to select specific sources such as a blog, podcast, or Web site and get summary or full text updates of content from the source. This increasingly popular mechanism enables users to subscribe to a specific "feed" or "channel" whose content is captured in XML, thereby customizing their RSS reader to individual interests.

An important research area is understanding how information flows among various media. For example, information posted on a Web page might subsequently be reposted on a blog and invoke discussion which might then be picked up as a story in a news site and eventually find its way to broadcast news. Understanding these often global flows is essential for modern public diplomacy.

Social Aspects of Media

Blogs and wikis represent a form of social media, media that enable groups to communicate or collaborate. Examples of social media include

- *Group authoring* (blogs, wikis);
- *Collaborative filtering* or recommender systems (Amazon, Movielens);
- *Social Networking* (MySpace, Facebook, LinkedIn);
- *Social bookmarking* (del.icio.us, Furl, Connotea); and
- *Collaborative annotation* (Flickr, IBM's dogear, MITRE's Onomi).

As might be expected, users exhibit social behavior in media. For example, according to Gladwell, some participants take on special roles.[8] These include *connectors* who are hubs in social networks, *mavens* who are experts (such as bloggers who publish information or detect misinformation), and *salespeople* who persuasively influence others, often subconsciously.

These individuals can wield disproportionate influence and cause "social epidemics," or sudden and often chaotic phase changes from one state to another (such as when a particular idea becomes viral). Finally, their contributions reflect the power law, which states that contribution is an inverse log scale (few contribute most content; many contribute little). For an example of the power law, search for "Green Zone" photographs at Flickr.com. Twenty-two photographers took 482 images of the Green

Zone in Baghdad. Most of those images (80 percent) came from only four photographers (18 percent of all photographers), consistent with a so-called 80-20 phenomena observed in social media. In fact, 40 percent came from just one individual. The average number of photos was twenty-two, and 80 percent of the photographers provided fewer than that. This Flickr example illustrates how a few productive or influential contributors dominate the information space.

> An important research area is understanding how information flows among various media. For example, information posted on a Web page might subsequently be reposted on a blog and invoke discussion which might then be picked up as a story in a news site and eventually find its way to broadcast news. Understanding these often global flows is essential for modern public diplomacy.

One important property of digital media is the degree of interactivity and citizen reporting that is enabled. Sometimes individual and group reactions to the news, such as the commentary that follows an article, are more interesting than the news itself. While this is a boon to free speech, these "conversations" often proceed unmoderated and unvalidated, which often means more authentic and useful audience feedback.

VIRAL IDEAS: INFECTIVE AND AFFECTIVE

Like a social system, social media reflect the attitudes of their contributors and also can serve to amplify and accelerate certain behaviors. For example, just as societies can suffer from pandemics, so too ideas can infect and affect audiences. An idea or story can be considered *viral* if it is both infective and affective. An *infective* idea rapidly propagates, passed on by recipients. Like traditional infections, idea propagation rates can be influenced by structure, in this case by such elements as social structure or media structure. For example, if the idea is communicated by a public figure or powerful individual, it may achieve a broader distribution. Similarly, as discussed above, connectors, hubs in social networks, can accelerate propagation. Equally, media can accelerate propagation. For example, political or social movements frequently use Web sites and blogs to disseminate information with an intention of broadcast news networks picking up and retransmitting messages with the hope of having them effect change. Often these messages are intentionally *affective*; that is, aimed not only at rationale appeal but also at emotional impacts such as surprise, disgust, or fear. Related, there is a branch of computer science that seeks to recognize and generate affect automatically.[9] Infective and affective ideas can spread rapidly, as quickly as a fad. A key limited resource in this process is human attention, which Davenport and Beck argue needs to be better managed, both by information producers and consumers.[10] Related, Joe Nye points out the implications in his paradox of plenty.[11] Because attention is a scarce resource, this drives such consequences as the need for credibility, reliable authority, and celebrity diplomacy.

IMPLICATIONS

There are a number of important possible consequences of new media and implications for global communications. Some of the more likely include:

Death of censorship. Given the proliferation of sources and communication channels and the rise of the citizen reporter, the ability of central governments to control information is becoming increasingly difficult. Having said that, controlled societies will continue to suppress communications. For example, in October 2007, Schwankert reported that China had blocked Google's YouTube, Wikipedia, and the British Broadcasting Corporation's news site, although the Google blog site Blogspot.com and some pictures from Yahoo Inc.'s Flickr photos were available. China regularly blocks access to Web sites that it finds objectionable, including those dealing with politically sensitive subjects. Its blocking technology is reportedly beyond simple domain restrictions and could target sub-domains. However, with continuous and rapid Internet expansion, protecting cyberborders will become increasingly challenging.

Death of distance. While the majority of events will remain local, the real-time, global reach afforded by combinations of modern media (such as Webcams, Web sites, blogs, satellite broadcasts) implies that all local communications can potentially have global implications.

Death of Time. Traditional media such as newspapers or broadcast news which operated on a daily cycle have been upstaged by online information services, which provide real-time information 24/7. Audiences now expect to get tailored news and information on demand, when, where, and how they want it.

Global Personal Coverage. Viewer expectations are for real time individualized news across the globe. This implies that media producers need to rapidly adapt to audience interests in order to maintain limited viewer attention.

Trust challenges. Hand-in-hand with the ease of information creation and dissemination comes the challenge of validation and verification of content and sources. Who do you trust and on what topic? Walter Lippmann recognized this in 1922 in *Public Opinion*, in which he noted,

"On all but a very few matters for short stretches of our lives, the utmost independence that we can exercise is to multiply the authorities to whom we give a friendly hearing. As congenital amateurs our quest for truth consists in stirring up the experts ..."[12]

Birth of new media forms. Media products and channels will continue to evolve and result in new forms such as satellite radio, podcasting, and virtual environments for communication and collaboration, such as Second Life.

Emergence of agile adversaries. Kimmage and Ridolfo describe how insurgents have learned to successfully exploit new media forms in a decentralized and flexible manner to promote viral ideas.[13] Using Web sites and television stations, Iraq's Sunni insurgency disseminates daily press releases, magazines, books, video clips, and films. This sophisticated media campaign leverages the Internet to target mainstream Arabic-language media, which can then amplify messages to a mass audience. Kimmage and Ridolfo also note, however, that decentralization has revealed disagreements between nationalist and global jihadist groups, which is a potential vulnerability.

Globalization and Regionalism. While language and cultural differences suggest the need for localization, reporting already transcends political boundaries and might be expected to continue. An alternative view argues for the continued economic, political, social, and media primacy of states, or, increasingly, of regions. An example of this is the remarkably rapid rise of Al Jazeera to become a pan-Arab news broadcaster of nearly 50 million viewers.

IMPLICATIONS FOR PUBLIC DIPLOMACY

These new media trends have a number of implications for public diplomacy. Just as Madison Avenue has developed methods such as audience analysis and targeted marketing to very successfully model and influence consumer behavior, so, too, governments need to skillfully leverage modern communications. This implies the need to develop a full-spectrum, sophisticated method of digital media management including a cycle of:

- *Production*, the ability to create factual but compelling stories that appeal to global audiences and at the same time connect to local concerns. Content will need to appeal not only to hearts and minds but also to universal values. In the terminology of Aristotle, it must ring true to *pathos* (emotion), *logos* (logic), and *ethos* (ethics).
- *Dissemination*, the ability to rapidly create media, synergistically across multiple infrastructures and languages, possibly

customized for multiple audiences. Careful attention should be paid to the credibility of the voice and channel. Traditional regional broadcasters (such as Al Jazeera and Al Arabiya) serve to keep the diaspora connected to their home societies.

- *Context*, the death of censorship, distance, and time increases the need for political, social, and historical framing of information that may arise from distant, unvetted, and real-time sources.
- *Tracking*, the ability to track audience attention, attitudes, and reactions in real time to both friendly and adversarial media.
- *Targeting*, the ability to understand the technical infrastructure and influence networks that support media.
- *Interdiction*, the ability to disrupt, refute, or discredit media networks that undermine universal values. This could start with simple methods such as is done in advertisement or campaign fact checking, or via sites that debunk myths or rumors.

In short, we need a process that takes advantage of the realities of our connected globe and modern communications mechanisms.

CONCLUSION

As stated in the introduction, media, and the information they convey, can be a force multiplier or a force divider. The rapid expansion of the Internet and broad availability of digital media have resulted in unprecedented communication possibilities that will favor the agile agent in our global village. While media promise to be an effective instrument in the war on poverty, ignorance, disease, and environmental degradation, they have been shown equally to be a favored asymmetric means of undermining public opinion by insurgents. A major future challenge will be to ensure that these new communication infrastructures, technologies, and systems best serve humankind.

Notes

1. Pew Internet and American Life Project, Associated Press, AOL cell phone survey. March 8–28, 2006.

2. www.aim.com/survey/#Mobile%20Messaging.

3. Coleman, A. BBC Monitoring Report from International Broadcasting Convention, Amsterdam, September 12, 2007.

4. Anthony Gidden, *Runaway World* (London: Routledge, 2000), 30. See also www. ecommerce.gov/emerging.htm/.

5.   Where Are My Listeners Going? Bridge Ratings Audience Erosion Study 2006- Q4 Update. October 27, 2006. Accessed November 27, 2007, from www.bridgeratings. com/press_Where%20Are%20Listeners%20Going%20Update.10.27.2006.htm/.

6.   Source:www.bridgeratings.com/press_031006-digitalprojectionsupdwradio.htm/.

7   J. Giles, "Internet encyclopedias go head to head," *Nature* 438 (2005): 900-901.

8.   M. Gladwell, *The Tipping Point: How Little Things Can Make a Big Difference* (Boston: Little, Brown, and Company, 2000).

9.   R. Picard, *Affective Computing* (Cambridge, MA: MIT Press, 1997).

10.   T. Davenport and J. Beck, *The Attention Economy: Understanding the New Currency of Business* (Cambridge: Harvard Business School Press, 2001).

11.   www.theglobalist.com/DBWeb/printStoryId.aspx?StoryId=3885.

12.   Walter Lippmann, *Public Opinion* (New York: Simon and Schuster, 1922), 143.

13.   D. Kimmage, and K. Ridolfo, "Iraqi Insurgent Media: The War of Images And Ideas" (Radio Free Europe/Radio Liberty, 2007). The report is available for download from www.rferl.org/featuresarticle/2007/06/830debc3-e399-4fa3-981c-cc44badae1a8. html/.

16. Digital Technology in Public Diplomacy

Adam Clayton Powell III

I'M A JOURNALIST WHO FINDS HIMSELF, to his surprise, a professor of engineering and, before June 2007, running a national engineering research laboratory. (Now, even more to my surprise, I'm a Vice Provost.) Our lab is the USC Integrated Media Systems Center. One hundred and eighteen universities competed for this federal designation and funding, and USC won; we just celebrated our tenth anniversary. Later, I will discuss some of the lab's research and describe some work that has not been seen in public on the East Coast (it has been seen at National Science Foundation presentations).

But first, I have been asked to talk about the future of international broadcasting and to guess what may lie ahead in the new media, what's "on the other side of the hill." We can start with what we know, which is:

In the beginning, there was shortwave, and it was good.

And then came AM and FM radio, and satellite radio, and satellite television, and they were good.

But they were all expensive. U.S. government–funded international broadcasting costs nearly $700 million a year these days. Yet some of the networks, which still spend most of their funds on radio, cannot afford to venture into expensive TV production.

So along comes the Internet, which is really good. And the best news is that it is really cheap.

We already have sixty languages, at last count, in international broadcasting under the aegis of the Broadcasting Board of Governors, most of them online. And one of the best things about the Internet is that you don't need anyone's permission to get on it: no licenses, no transmitters, no frequencies. You just start doing it.

In the early 1990s, U.S. international broadcasters were the first to use the Internet, along with the Communications Research Centre in Canada.

Adam Clayton Powell III is vice provost for globalization at the University of Southern California Center on Public Diplomacy.

And now we have television on the Internet, and because of that, we see an incredible fragmentation of audiences. To illustrate what is happening, let's take the case of Al Jazeera English. Major cable providers in the United States have refused to carry this new service launched in late 2006. So what is Al Jazeera English, which reaches much of the rest of the world, doing?

They are transmitting their 24/7 service over the Internet, along with a few digital satellite feeds. This is an example of international broadcaster transmitting television but, in effect, bypassing "broadcast" television.

Germany's overseas radio and television network, Deutsche Welle, gives an annual award for Weblogs, and the contest attracted an entry from the United States, from the Sunlight Foundation.[1] It's a rather interesting blog that resembles something that might be presented by a U.S. international broadcaster. It's basically news and information, but a very different mix, and in a format that is quite popular in the blogosphere.

In the Arab world, blogs are becoming very important. According to recent data from Internet World Stats, 13.5 percent of the Arab world now has Internet access, a sixteen-fold increase since 2000, and growing.[2] The number of bloggers in Saudi Arabia alone tripled during the first ten months of 2006. So blogs are an international medium, or sub-medium, which is starting to take off.

You can now watch *Meet the Press* or NBC Nightly News on podcast.[3] CBS has been transmitting the CBS Evening News live on the Internet. Podcasts are definitely coming, even to seatback screens on airplanes: take your iPod on a plane and plug it into an outlet on the seat in front of you.

iPods can also be used for education. iTunesU is one of the latest aggregators. Stanford, Michigan, and a number of other universities actually put their course materials, lectures, and notes online. A medium usually associated with music has now become an educational information provider. And if you think iPods are just the rage here in America, my friends in Africa are emailing me, "Next time you come to Africa, bring us iPods."

How many of you have visited YouTube?[4] What's happening now is that some companies are actually starting to post things on YouTube as part of marketing and part of market tests. And we know what happened to some political candidates in the 2006 election, one in particular in Virginia, when material was posted on YouTube.

You may or may not have visited Second Life, but you have almost certainly read about it.[5] It's a 3-D virtual world, live, 24/7. Some public diplomacy events have already taken place there. USC has bought an island on Second Life, an island where we can present lectures and other events. Look at the number of residents in this virtual world: 1,409,000. And from the emails we get from events we do on Second Life, we know that they're all over the world. So again, here we have something very new, which few anticipated.

CNN posted an article about educational applications, describing how universities are starting to offer lectures that you can attend in Second Life.[6] It's attracting so much attention, they're now worried about virtual thieves robbing people in a virtual world—and not many people ever considered that as a threat.

And if you think Second Life is mainly about entertainment, consider this: Reuters has just opened a news bureau there, and the wire service is actually filing stories about events in Second Life. The events are not real, not tangible, but now they are news. It's really quite remarkable.

Diplomats have already embraced Second Life and other social network sites. In 2007, Sweden and the Maldives even opened virtual embassies there, perhaps suggesting a way the United States could reduce those long lines for visas and other consular services at the real-world embassies. The social networking site MySpace at one point in 2006 could claim to be the most popular Web destination for Americans,[7] and by mid-2007 had settled down with 55 million unique visitors per month,[8] a collection of visitors larger than the entire populations of South Korea, South Africa or Spain. Facebook, another popular site, had more than 19 million unique visitors a month by mid-2007, roughly the population of Syria.[9]

Then there is YouTube: The on-demand Internet video service logged over 57 million unique visitors in October 2007, according to Nielsen Netratings.[10] That was more than the number of people who logged in at Amazon or eBay. YouTube and the other Web video sites are no longer small niches, and because they can be seen and heard worldwide, there is no question they are in fact international broadcasters.

One dramatic example was provided when video from Burma was distributed over the Internet, posted on such sites as BurmaNet and then used on television by the BBC and other broadcasters. Eventually, to try to stem the flow of unofficial news, the Burmese military closed off the Internet and even the mobile phone network,[11] but that is an option available only to countries with isolated and undeveloped economies, such as Burma or North Korea.

Another new medium is video games, and the massive multi-player games are enormously popular around the world. We may still think of them as entertainment, with games such as "Grand Theft Auto." But now many video games are educational.[12]

Video games are also now a tool for public diplomacy. USC sponsored a contest for the best public diplomacy video game, which was won by a peace game constructed at another university. A runner up was a game built by kids who were so young they had to be brought by chaperones.

Diplomats have already embraced Second Life and other social network sites. In 2007, Sweden and the Maldives even opened virtual embassies there, perhaps suggesting a way the U.S. could reduce those long lines for visas and other consular services at the real-world embassies.

We should take note that the virtual world is also a place where people are making political statements. Here is one example: some players went into the Pentagon's "America's Army" video game and held a protest there against the Iraq war.[13]   Remember, this was inside a game, "America's Army." This demonstrates the range of political speech and range of public diplomacy communications that we already have. These all present opportunities for public diplomacy, opportunities that were inconceivable just a few years ago.

Finally, there is one tool that is quite dramatic. We're not sure quite where it fits in public diplomacy, but former Undersecretary of State Karen Hughes traveled to USC and has seen this. Perhaps it fits into cultural exchanges, or perhaps it is the future news and information. Some industry partners in this particular research are Microsoft and Google, and they are developing their own versions that will soon be publicly available. All information and images that are available to and used by this tool are publicly available on the Internet.

We begin with an aerial view of the USC campus, constructed from two publicly available satellite views of Los Angeles, to get depth. Next, USC's software actually corrects online maps and other data to the presumably accurate satellite imagery. As you zoom in, there is additional height information available, and you can access live online information and live GPS data about the exact location where you are zooming.

Now you can see the software querying databases it is finding, databases related to the exact address or GPS location that you have chosen to pinpoint. For example, it can find names of buildings and streets. But go closer, and you can see it insert a live video picture, "painted" into the 3-D model. So, if you're online live looking at the plaza in front of our lab building, looking down the street, you can actually watch and follow somebody walking down the sidewalk or follow someone driving a car. The resolution isn't quite good enough to read license plates, but that's coming. And this is a stripped down version of what can be done, not in five years, not in three years, but today.

Another example is in Washington, D.C. We constructed a model of the area between 15th Street and Union Station. We constructed the model in about two hours (now it takes just an hour) and then inserted live video feeds, and you can see it in a clip posted on MSNBC.[14]

Given that there are thousands of video cameras in many cities—think of all of the security cameras in London!—you can stitch these images together to create a live, high-resolution, 3-D view of a neighborhood or an entire city. And by the way, it's possible to record and save past offerings. You can in effect TiVo downtown Washington, DC. You want to see the intersection of 14th Street and Pennsylvania Avenue at 3:35 A.M. last Tuesday? No problem: just go in and zoom around the 3-D image to watch who was there and what they were doing.

But what does this have to do with public diplomacy?

Think of this as a tool waiting to be used. We don't know what applications might evolve. For example, consider the inventor of the screwdriver. The screwdriver makes many things possible, far beyond the wildest dreams of the tool's inventor. The same thing will happen with these digital tools now being invented.

One way to think about these new tools is to take an historical view. Perhaps digital technology can be the new jazz of public diplomacy.

Fifty years ago, Dizzy Gillespie and his band toured the Middle East, Africa, and Latin America, going to places where they were storming U.S. embassies and hanging President Eisenhower in effigy. They hated American foreign policy, but they all ran to the Dizzy Gillespie concert. It was a way of turning some of America's enemies into, if not friends, then at least fans.

At USC, we recently celebrated the fiftieth anniversary of that tour in an event that was opened by the Secretary of State, on video from Washington. We also invited members of the orchestra who actually made that tour, starting with the musical director of Dizzy Gillespie band of 1956, a young trumpeter named Quincy Jones. Quincy came to the celebration, along with a pianist they picked up in Buenos Aires, a musician named Lalo Schifrin. Lalo played a piano solo, and if you think an 80-year-old pianist cannot make really great music on the keyboard, think again: he was really terrific. You can hear some of it in a story that ran on NPR.[15]

We also captured the music and the discussion led by Geoff Cowan, former director of VOA, recorded using HD video and USC's immersive audio format, which is also accommodated in the new digital cinema standard. And we will work to make that all available, and perhaps that is a twenty-first century re-purposing of mid-twentieth century public diplomacy.

We call this family of technologies "immersive presence," and it represents a tool for collaboration or virtual cultural exchange that can be part of cultural diplomacy of the future. Maybe some day it will even be called international broadcasting.

Notes

1. www.sunlightfoundation.com/blog.

2. Calculated from data found on www.internetworldstats.com/, January 5, 2008.

3. "NBC News Launches Video Podcasts," November 13, 2006, www.msnbc.msn.com/id/15699236. Accessed November 25, 2007.

4. www.youtube.com/.

5. secondlife.com/.

6. Grace Wong, "Educators Explore Second Life," CNN, November 14, 2006, www.cnn.com/2006/TECH/11/13/second.life.university/index.html. Accessed November 25, 2007.

7. Marshall Kirkpatrick, "MySpace hit #1 US destinatin last week, Hitwise," July 11, 2006, www.techcrunch.com/2006/07/11/myspace-hit-1-us-destination-last-week-hitwise/. Accessed November 25, 2007.

8. Michael Arrington, "MySpace/Photobucket: User Overlap is Nearly 100%," May 7, 2007, www.techcrunch.com/2007/05/07/myspacephotobucket-user-overlap-is-nearly-100/. Accessed November 25, 2007.

9. www.nielsen-netratings.com/pr/pr_070920.pdf.

10. www.nielsen-netratings.com/pr/pr_071112.pdf.

11. Mick Elmore, "Myanmar Blocks Internet, Cuts Off Phones," Associated Press, September 28, 2007, www.sfgate.com/cgi-bin/article.cgi?f=/n/a/2007/09/28/international/i093232D95.DTL&tsp=1. Accessed November 25, 2007.

12. Ben Feller, "Scientists: Video games can reshape education," Associated Press, October 17, 2006, online at www.usatoday.com/tech/gaming/2006-10-17-gaming-education_x.htm. Accessed November 25, 2007.

13. Rebecca Clarren, "Virtually dead in Iraq," *Salon*, September 16, 2006, online at www.salon.com/ent/feature/2006/09/16/americasarmy/. Accessed November 25, 2007.

14. Alan Boyle, "Virtual world meets the real world," www.msnbc.msn.com/id/12482125/. Accessed November 25, 2007.

15. Karen Grigsby Bates, "Dizzy Gillespie's Cold War Jazz Diplomacy," www.npr.org/templates/story/story.php?storyId=6276832. Accessed November 25, 2007.

17. Sesame Workshop: Beyond Borders

Gary E. Knell

On May 9, 1961, Newton Minow made a speech to the National Association of Broadcasters that underscored the state of the quality of television programming. Minow said, "When television is good, nothing—not the theater, not the magazines or newspapers—nothing is better. But when television is bad, nothing is worse. I invite you to sit down in front of your television set … I can assure you that you will observe a vast wasteland."[1] Over half a century later, the growth of media outlets and the exchange of information and technologies is making our world smaller and opening the media landscape. In a multi-channel environment and with numerous media choices, the wasteland has dramatically grown. But despite the dismal outlook that Minow set forth, Sesame Workshop is reaching out beyond our borders to harness the power of media and create content that can bridge gaps and make a positive impact.

A few years after Minow's landmark words were spoken, a group of people came together not only answering the call for better quality programming but also to do something previously untried: to use television as a tool to teach. Early research on the way children viewed television showed that they could remember advertising jingles better than information in the programs they viewed. A public affairs producer, Joan Ganz Cooney, and a foundation executive, Lloyd Morrisett, pulled together a team of comedy writers, TV producers, and educators to experiment with the idea that if children could remember jingles, they could most likely learn other important and more useful information if presented in a similar manner.

They set out to use television to help children, particularly at-risk inner city kids, to enter school ready to learn and to channel their natural attraction to TV in a positive and purposeful way. They created a revolutionary program, somewhat modeled after *Rowan & Martin's Laugh-In*, called *Sesame Street*.

Gary E. Knell is president and chief executive officer of Sesame Workshop.

Sesame Street instantly stood out because of the way it was designed, a typical urban city street inhabited by people and furry monsters of all different shapes, colors, and ethnicities that reflects the realities of life to help children understand everyday situations that they might encounter in their own lives. In addition to teaching letters and numbers, this neighborhood reflected the same kinds of family events kids and parents experience.

Nearly four decades later, the experiment continues and has extended to over 120 countries, making *Sesame Street* "the longest street in the world." Using the same model *Sesame Street* was built on, Sesame Workshop has created local coproductions of the show in over thirty countries. The Workshop collaborates with local educators and researchers to develop a curriculum and works with local producers, writers, musicians, actors and puppeteers to create impactful programs that are locally accepted and welcomed in each country they are produced in. Each program captures the fun and essence of the original program while depicting the unique culture of the country and catering to the educational needs of each audience. These productions go beyond teaching letters and numbers, taking on complex and often difficult subjects such as respect and understanding, in the context of our times, with insight and sensitivity.

For instance, in South Africa, where one in nine children are HIV-positive, Sesame Workshop and its partners, the South African Broadcasting Corporation, Sanlam, Department of Education, United States Agency for International Development, and Kwasukasukela, decided to use the series *Takalani Sesame* (*Be Happy Sesame*) as a vehicle to address stigma and the discrimination associated with HIV/AIDS. Kami, an HIV-positive five-year-old girl Muppet whose mother died of AIDS has been helping these children deal with the stigma they face. She is a UNICEF Champion for Children and has opened a dialogue where millions have been ignored due to the stigma surrounding the disease.

In Egypt, where 60 percent of the female population is illiterate, the show *Alam Simsim* (*Sesame World*) is providing positive role models in characters like Khokha and her friends, who encourage girls to aspire to higher learning and careers. The show has started over a million children on the road to literacy and numeracy, fosters knowledge of health and hygiene, celebrates Egyptian culture, and encourages a positive self-image.

With its growing importance on the world stage and a population of 128 million children between the ages of two and six, Sesame Workshop is making a difference through a local Sesame project in India. *Galli Galli Sim Sim* (*Little Sesame Streets*) illustrates the Workshop's mission at work and celebrates India's vibrant culture using uniquely adapted content, original Muppet characters, and a diverse human cast that represent the commonalities and diversity of children growing up in India. The program transcends socioeconomic barriers encouraging education for all children.

A *Galli Galli Sim Sim* outreach initiative was launched simultaneously with the on-air launch of the series. With millions of people who do not have regular access to television, the initiative, funded by the

> Our world knows no technological boundaries or borders, and cultures, religions, and ethnicities intersect in ways previously undreamt.

Michael and Susan Dell Foundation, extends the reach and impact of *Galli Galli Sim Sim* to underserved communities and elevates the importance of early childhood development and education in India. So far, the mobile vans showing the program have reached over 55,000 children and 18,000 caregivers in Delhi and Mumbai.

The Workshop has also worked in many conflicted regions for decades. Today, programs air in Israel, Palestine, Jordan, and Kosovo. In 2008, a new production will air in Northern Ireland. Through these programs, we strive to develop self-esteem, empathy, and understanding, and hopefully to open children's and parents' minds by humanizing "the other side." With casts of Muppets and humans, along with images that depict children like themselves, we aim to show the similarities we share but also the differences that make our world distinct.

Our world knows no technological boundaries or borders, and cultures, religions, and ethnicities intersect in ways previously undreamt. The images we share and the stories we tell have the ability to both reflect and shape reality and the potential to extend far beyond the television set, especially with children, who have a natural attraction to media. The Workshop's experience continues to see doors opening across the globe in sharing information and technologies. There is no better time to support new efforts that challenge existing limitations and take advantage of the substantial strengths that all forms of media have to offer and partnering locally with producers and experts to create indigenously relevant, inspiring content. Media alone cannot solve the many problems of the world but, we do believe that it would be a terrible mistake not to use these influential tools to contribute to building bridges, finding solutions, and transforming "the wasteland" into a valuable resource.

Notes

1. "'Vast Wasteland' Speech Holds True After All These Years," *Chicago Tribune*, April 24, 2001, 17.

PART 6
A VISION FOR THE FUTURE

18. The BBG Global Strategy

James K. Glassman

Since 1942, when the Voice of America (VOA) was launched to combat the Nazi threat, U.S. international broadcasting has been an effective means of advancing America's strategic interests to support freedom and democracy around the world.

During the Cold War, VOA and Radio Free Europe and Radio Liberty (RFE/RL) broadcasts conveyed accurate and comprehensive news, information, and ideas to the peoples of the former Soviet Union. They did so with creativity and aplomb, using the leading communication and broadcasting techniques of the day, including a wide range of cultural programming and music. Willis Conover's jazz show on VOA was not only great entertainment for music-starved listeners in the Communist bloc but also a symbol of the creative freedom of liberal democracies.

The broadcasts were hugely successful: survey research among émigrés and travelers supported the anecdotal evidence and pointed to high weekly listening rates, often one-third or more of the adult populations. Polish leader Lech Walesa compared RFE/RL to the sun for the role it played in shedding light on the reality of life in Poland.

Building on the earlier successes of VOA and RFE/RL, Radio and TV Marti made their debut in the 1980s to inform Cubans oppressed by the Castro regime in Cuba. Radio Free Asia arose in the aftermath of Tiananmen Square in China.

The times today are different from those during the Cold War and even the 1990s. So are the target audiences and the communication techniques and technologies. But the fundamental principle underlying U.S. international broadcasting remains the same: a free press is essential to freedom.

Since the terrorist attacks of 9/11, the Broadcasting Board of Governors (BBG) has operated against the backdrop of two major national security concerns. The first is the authoritarianism that persists in many quarters

James K. Glassman is chairman, U.S. Broadcasting Board of Governors.

of the world, in North Korea, Cuba, Russia, China, Belarus, among others. The second is the rising extremism that 9/11 represented, a transnational phenomenon deeply rooted in many countries of the Middle East, Iran, Somalia, and others. In many places, authoritarianism and extremism are intertwined.

U.S. international broadcasting is playing a critical role to counter these threats. New broadcasting services developed by the BBG since 9/11 include Radio Sawa and Alhurra TV in Arabic for the Middle East, Radio Farda and expanded VOA TV in Persian for Iran, Aap ki Dunyaa Radio and TV in Urdu for Pakistan, a joint RFE/RL–VOA 24/7 programming stream to Afghanistan, and a host of additional new broadcasting programs and content streams for countries like Indonesia, Nigeria, and Somalia. Collectively, this new broadcasting has boosted the BBG's global audience levels from 100 million to 155 million in the past six years. Alhurra now draws more weekly viewers in Iraq than Al Jazeera.[1]

THE BROADCASTING BOARD OF GOVERNORS

The Broadcasting Board of Governors is the independent federal agency that oversees the civilian international broadcasting funded by the U.S. government. The BBG comprises three key components:

1. The broadcasting organizations, including the VOA, RFE/RL, the Middle East Broadcasting Networks (MBN) Alhurra TV and Radio Sawa, the Office of Cuba Broadcasting (OCB) Radio and TV Marti, and Radio Free Asia (RFA);

2. The operational support arm, in the form of the International Broadcasting Bureau (IBB), which provides personnel and administrative services for VOA, OCB, and the Board, as well as transmission and marketing support for all the broadcasters; and

3. The head of agency, the Board itself, a nine-member, part-time, bipartisan body of eight private citizens and the Secretary of State (*ex officio*), served by an executive director and other professional staff for strategic, budgetary, legal, and other operational support and oversight.

The BBG is one of the largest newsgathering and reporting operations in the world. It distributes content in sixty languages targeted to some seventy-five countries on an annual budget of $668 million. The BBG employs over 3,400 journalists, producers, technicians, and support personnel in headquarters in Washington (for VOA, IBB, RFA, and the

Board), Miami (for OCB), and Prague, Czech Republic (for RFE/RL) as well as some ninety news bureaus and offices worldwide. Correspondents and stringer reporters number an additional 3,000.

The BBG mission reflects our specific mandates from Congress: to promote freedom and democracy and to enhance understanding through multimedia communication of accurate, objective, and balanced news, information, and other programming about America and the world to audiences overseas.

While the core purpose is to be a free press in countries that do not have a free press, the BBG is concerned with enhancing the understanding of our audiences; that is, their understanding of their own political, economic, and social affairs; of key concepts such as the rule of law, human rights, and civil society; and, equally important, of U.S. policies, actions, and culture.

Yet, the BBG's role is not advocacy or overt persuasion. Other U.S. government public diplomacy and strategic communication programs at the State Department and elsewhere take on that role. We hew closely to our core competency of professional, objective journalism.

When VOA first went on the air, in German, in 1942, it did so with the pledge: "The news may be good. The news may be bad. We shall tell you the truth." This has been the credo of U.S. international broadcasting ever since and animates the work of BBG journalists today.

To meet the many challenges facing U.S. international broadcasting today, the BBG is pursuing a new global strategy for 2008-2013. Selected elements are highlighted below.

Enhancing Program Delivery across All Relevant Platforms
The single greatest challenge we face is to ensure effective distribution. Many of the countries to which the BBG broadcasts try to jam our direct broadcasts, limit or prohibit local distribution via affiliates, enforce laws that restrict broadcast content, and block our Internet sites. We also continue an intricate, complex internal transition from traditional shortwave transmission to distribution via television (free-to-air, cable, and satellite), FM, AM, the Internet, and other emerging technologies.

There is no one solution. Take-up rates for new media even in remote corners of the world are expanding, yet shortwave radio will remain a valuable delivery means for the foreseeable future. The right distribution is a market-by-market determination.

The BBG has been very successful in recent years in securing effective program delivery for new broadcasting initiatives in Iran, the Middle East, and elsewhere. But doing so for all language services remains a significant challenge. The BBG will therefore ensure that across the board our broadcasters' content is available via the media, bands, networks, channels, and stations our audiences actually use, either through direct broadcast or via affiliates.

Building on Our Reach and Impact within the Muslim World

Since 2001, the BBG has taken major strides toward better reaching the Muslim world, launching 24/7 broadcasting and other smaller initiatives valued collectively at more than $125 million annually. All told, these new services have gained the BBG some 40 million additional weekly listeners and viewers. Beyond the success stories mentioned above, there are further audiences in the Muslim world to be reached, and the BBG will act assertively to serve them. At the same time, U.S. broadcasters will continue to broaden and deepen the substance of their services to meet the needs of Muslim audiences not only for news and information but also for debate, discussion, and dialogue.

Helping Audiences in Authoritarian Countries Understand the Principles and Practices of Democratic, Free, and Just Societies

Recalcitrant authoritarianism persists into the twenty-first century. China and Russia are the two largest examples, and North Korea represents one of the most dangerous cases and a pressing U.S. national security imperative. Yet there are other offenders. Reaching audiences in these and other authoritarian countries will continue to be a BBG priority.

Employing Modern Communication Techniques and Technologies

By mandate from Congress, BBG broadcasts must "be designed so as to effectively reach a significant audience." Media competition continues to diversify and intensify, fragmenting market share and increasingly necessitating customized local strategies and expert implementation to maintain and enhance competitiveness. Broadcast and computer technologies are leaping forward. Audiences' increasing demand for service across platforms necessitates the development of new product as well as state-of-the-art news-gathering and production techniques. People also increasingly want greater dialogue and interactivity. This is especially true for VOA audiences, who seek a conversation with America.

The BBG must do more than stay abreast of emerging technologies; it must be on the cutting edge. The BBG's successful "marry the mission to the market" approach, in place since 2002, will continue to guide efforts to adopt formats and delivery means consistent with local circumstances and audience needs. The aim is to expand audience reach while preserving the core mission of distributing factual news and information.

Facilitating Citizen Discourse

While many governments continue to stifle freedom of expression in all forms (and specifically seek to block U.S. international broadcasting), technology is nonetheless empowering unprecedented participatory discourse among ordinary citizens. Widespread access to PCs, the Internet, and cell phones, coupled with email, chat rooms, and blogs, is creating dramatically new information flows.

Savvy media today work hand in glove with this development by providing news and information that feeds citizen discourse and by offering new channels for citizens to engage in discussion (for example, the growing number of media-sponsored blogs and interactive channels).

BBG services have a special role to play by helping to open up these new channels of communication in relatively less well-developed information environments. We also have an important comparative advantage by often being among the few, credible news sources in many vernacular languages. Thus, we see a growing opportunity to fulfill our core mission by democratizing information exchange and discourse.

Engaging the World in Conversation about America

Helping audiences understand clearly what America stands for—our principles and our people—is essential. The position and policies of America in the world today inspire strong international reaction. This helps drive desire among millions of people to seek a conversation with America. But it also places a special burden on us as communicators to connect with audiences that now might not be predisposed to tuning us in. International opinion polls, and our own research, suggest that dialogue not monologue will be among our best means of reaching people. Meeting this demand for dialogue is thus a strategic opportunity and a mission imperative, especially for the VOA.

Rationalizing the Broadcasting Enterprise

Rationalizing U.S. international broadcasting following the end of the Cold War was a main impetus behind the 1994 U.S. International Broadcasting Act and the creation of the Board. The Board has acted to consolidate global transmissions and program delivery and has eliminated or reduced lower priority language services and expanded higher priority services. The Board will continue to evaluate options to realign the Agency's assets to meet the mission in the most effective and efficient manner possible. This evaluation will incorporate annual language service review, proposals for restructuring, and input from the Government Accountability Office, Office of Management and Budget, and Congress.

MEASURING SUCCESS

The BBG is keen to regularly assess how many people are using our services and what they think of our news and information. To have any impact at all, we must first reach significant audiences, and those audiences need to believe what we tell them. We know from our long history that there has never been an instance of democratization in a country reached by our broadcasts where we did not enjoy a mass audience.

> Is democratic change going to happen over night? No. Is sustaining such targeted journalistic activity critical to do regardless how long change takes? Yes.

Measures of success should match the organizational mission. For the BBG, that means ultimately seeing concrete change on the ground in terms of greater freedom, democracy, and openness. But, as in the Cold War, that success is often recognized only after the fact.

Before closed societies break wide open, there are almost always preliminary signs of transformation: Buddhist monks demonstrating in the streets of Rangoon against the military regime of Burma, where VOA and RFA have a 20 percent combined weekly reach; or striking bus drivers protesting amid a police crackdown in Iran, covered by the country's most popular foreign radio station, Radio Farda, which broadcast the event using live cell phone reports from citizen journalists; or a prominent general in Venezuela dissenting from the Hugo Chavez regime in an exclusive interview for VOA's Spanish service, one of the few remaining independent voices reaching the Venezuelan people.

These are instances of interim success. Is democratic change going to happen over night? No. Is sustaining such targeted journalistic activity critical to do regardless how long change takes? Yes.

The BBG is constantly refining its performance indicators. Audience reach and news reliability are not sufficient to fully assess our performance and impact in influencing the democratization process. The mission emphasis on enhancing understanding is driving more sophisticated quantitative and qualitative research and analysis of the effects of our broadcasting.

To sum up: the leadership of the BBG envisions a U.S. international broadcasting enterprise that is increasingly effective in reaching significant audiences in countries that deny, or lack the means to provide, their citizens access to factual, balanced news and information. It will also be an organization that is increasingly streamlined, coordinated, and efficient. The strategies reviewed above speak to the ways in which we intend to accomplish these aims.

Notes

1. "InterMedia, Iraq National Survey on Media Consumption, Washington, D.C.: September 2007. Estimates derived from the Iraq National Survey on Media Consumption, September 2007, of the adult population 15+. At the 95 percent confidence level, the estimate for Al Jazeera weekly viewers is 52.63 percent with a standard error of 2.31 and margin of error of 4.53, and the estimate for Alhurra weekly viewers is 55.58 percent with a standard error of 3.11 and margin of error of 6.10.

19. Broadcasting Lessons from the Cold War

Kevin Klose

LATE IN THE AFTERNOON of March 20, 1993, Mikhail S. Gorbachev motored through Moscow to the historic Central House of Writers, an ornate art nouveau manor house not far from the Kremlin. A gathering place of writers since czarist times, the Tsentralnyi Dom Literatorov during the Soviet era had been notorious for bitter political and propaganda intrigues powered by the police state's drive to censor thought, speech, and song throughout the Communist empire.

But this day, it was the site of something very different indeed: a celebration of the fortieth anniversary of the Russian language broadcasts of Radio Liberty (RL), the private shortwave service organized and supported throughout the Cold War by the U.S. government to bring uncensored news about the USSR to its citizens.

Gorbachev, reviled by his countrymen as the man who lost the Soviet empire, was intent upon showing yet again his determination to think and act differently. He joined the mixed throng of Russians and Americans gathered in the writers' den. Amid tables of zakuski and glasses of mineral water, wine, and champagne, Gorbachev told us that since he was now in the opposition, he listened to RL Russian Service "every day."

Calling the radio service a "stabilizing influence in an unstable time," the fallen Soviet president said, "I hope to be present at the fiftieth anniversary of Radio Liberty in 2003!" Applause greeted these words of support from the man who had done so much to dissolve the Communist empire. In the crowd were scores of Russian writers and artists whose works, banned by Soviet censors, had been smuggled out of the USSR over the years and broadcast back into the empire by RL's Russian Service. Among the Americans witnessing this remarkable event and enjoying it immensely were Eugene Pell, president of Radio Free Europe/Radio Liberty (RFE/RL)

Kevin Klose, president of National Public Radio (1998-present), was associate director of the U.S. Information Agency/director of U.S. International Broadcasting (1997-98); president of Radio Free Europe/Radio Liberty (1994-97); and director of Radio Liberty (1992-94).

for nearly a decade; and Malcolm S. Forbes, multi-millionaire publisher of one of capitalism's most successful business news empires, who was a close friend of Pell's and chairman of the Radios' board of directors.

Later that night, the anniversary celebration culminated with a pageant of poems, songs, and dramatic sketches staged and performed by the Russian Service's producers and writers, and featuring the works of the long-suppressed artists. The festivities ended when the auditorium audience was asked to stand and join together to sing "America, the Beautiful." It was a sublime moment for Radio Liberty.

Perhaps more than any other aspect of the celebration, Gorbachev's salute marked the symbolic end of the greatest and most successful effort up to that time to project democratic ideas—tolerance; equality; self-rule; and freedoms of conscience, assembly, and speech—across a vast region where these principles were suppressed, along with those who dared espouse them.

In a larger sense, Gorbachev's was a declaration made on behalf of all the radios of the Western Alliance that, together with RL, had broadcast into the USSR and its East European buffer states throughout the Cold War: Radio Free Europe, RL's twin surrogate service to Central and Eastern Europe; the Voice of America (VOA), founded in 1942 a few weeks after Pearl Harbor; the BBC, mission-parent of all such services; Deutsche Welle, the German Wave; Radio France Internationale; services from Scandinavia, Holland, and Canada; and smaller radio stations as well from Luxembourg, and elsewhere. All aimed at telling truth to power within a closed, guarded, empire of one-party police states.

In the years since, the revolutionary power of the worldwide Internet, together with the development of new platforms for digital communications, have transformed the world of international democracy-supporting programming services, even as the East-West divide fractured into an asymmetrical confrontation and crisis between the United States and the world of al-Qaeda and its allies. The stalwart standard-bearers of the Western Alliance—BBC, VOA, RFE/RL, Deutsche Welle, RFI, Radio Canada International—are struggling every day to adapt to a new world of infinitely greater complexity. The political division of the industrial world into pro-Western, pro-Communist, and neutral countries is long gone. The East-West divide is no longer solely about Washington and its allies vs. Moscow and its allies. The very asymmetry of the current confrontation among the United States and al-Qaeda and similar terrorist organizations challenge the West's centralized program services in ways unimagined in 1993. Back then, it seemed as if the long postwar struggle could give way to a new era of international cooperation, perhaps the "sunlit uplands"

Churchill had suggested in his memorable "Their Finest Hour" speech to the Commons back in 1940.

Indeed, less than two years after Gorbachev's visit to the fortieth anniversary celebration, Radio Free Europe/Radio Liberty narrowly averted being silenced for good, near victims of the search in post-Cold War America for an elusive "peace dividend" to be repaid after the decades of armed, watchful tensions and vigilance between East and West. To avert the budget axe, RFE/RL was radically downsized, uprooted from its longtime programming center in Munich, and moved quickly to Prague, the Czech Republic, achieving significant cost reductions and greater relevance in the newly democratizing Central Europe.

Today, like other major Cold War radio services, RFE/RL is still broadcasting in multiple languages to Eurasia, seeking to use the proven power of democratic ideas and ideals to embed themselves in the lives and aspirations of millions of people in some of the most remote and closed countries of the world.

Similar challenges and changes enveloped all the international services that once aimed much of their programming at the Soviet bloc. Throughout the 1990s, many faced severe budget reductions and a decline in focus. And then came the terrible attacks of 9/11, plunging the United States into a dangerous, complex new conflict. The broadcasters have struggled ever since to combat virulent anti-American, anti-Western polemics and propaganda dispensed worldwide through state-of-the-art satellite and Internet services. The U.S. effort, dogged early on by bitter controversies over content and relevance that centered on Alhurra TV and Radio Sawa, is now bringing increasing innovation to the multimedia, multi-platform digital media world; funding can likely rise as the broadcasters reinvent themselves and show credible gains in reaching long-neglected new listeners across the new arc of confrontation.

The combination of FM retransmission from satellites, Internet streaming, podcasts, and even hourly headlines and other brief segments tailored to cell phone services has brought the services into contact with important new audiences and user groups. The "surrogate" approach to broadcasting, which seeks to develop in-country reporting to create a viable alternate—and uncensored—news source in information-deprived states is as relevant today as during the Cold War. News from America that goes behind the headlines to tell the deeper narratives of a nation that struggles constantly with its own imperfections has special value for millions who have been told a very different story about the United States. The power of the digital revolution to connect people instantaneously around the globe means that broadcasters will do best when they move quickly and thoughtfully to take advantage of the new media's self-empowerment and "witnessing" potential. The future demands that the one-to-all broadcast paradigm shift to a model of all-to-all interactivity, which will engender comprehension, connection, and ultimately, change.

> The future demands that the one-to-all broadcast paradigm shift to a model of all-to-all interactivity, which will engender comprehension, connection, and ultimately, change.

As the global Internet community expands, very important steps are being taken by a wide array of media and Web-based organizations—from YouTube to human rights groups to international broadcasters—to reach out to digital-savvy activists in the closed societies of this new era. International broadcasters find many indigenous, spontaneously created, voluntary networks of determined citizens with camcorders, flash recorders, cell phones, and Internet services. International radio, TV, and the global Internet facilitate the fusing of international and indigenous witnessing. Videos of Buddhist monks being beaten by police in Myanmar, the exposure of police brutality in Egypt through spontaneous interviews with bloggers about their startling videos of beatings in jails, instant global access to crackdowns against opposition rallies in China, Russia, and elsewhere are the vital new ingredients in the new age of interactive international broadcasting.

But what is not new is the continuing commitment in the best-run international services to focus their efforts—as in earlier times—on the ideas of democracy, self-government, equality, and human freedoms. According to Mark Rhodes, founding president of InterMedia Survey, new data gathered and analyzed by his Washington-based international audience service indicates a global audience of "155 million unduplicated listeners, viewers and/or visitors weekly" to the U.S. government's civilian external broadcasters.[1] Many of these listeners live in scores of countries where their individual freedoms are no less repressed than were those of Soviet citizens through much of the past century. In serving these oppressed peoples of the post-Cold War world, America's international radios will do their best when they bear witness to those who aspire to the freedoms that we Americans all too often take for granted.

This can be accomplished if the nation's international broadcasting services are funded thoughtfully and generously, supported by a new bipartisan Congressional coalition similar to the postwar core of Republicans and Democrats who nurtured the broadcast services throughout the Cold War, and encouraged to find the best and brightest minds of the multimedia era to bring the full powers of the digital revolution into the global struggle for individual liberties.

Notes

1. Author interview with Mark Rhodes, January 7, 2008.

20. ROUNDTABLE: AMBASSADOR WILLIAM A. RUGH AND INTERNATIONAL BROADCASTING BUREAU RESEARCH SPECIALIST DR. KIM ANDREW ELLIOTT
October 2007

Moderator: Alan L. Heil Jr.

HEIL: The first question is the one that many people ask: should the U.S. government be involved in U.S. international broadcasting at all, why or why not?

RUGH: Well, I think definitely, yes. The international communication environment has expanded dramatically and the increase in voices around the world hasn't necessarily been universally helpful to the United States in presenting an accurate, balanced, and fair picture of America and its policies. And if we are not participating in that discussion, we are abdicating our responsibility to engage others in a dialogue. I think the U.S. government must be involved, and has a responsibility to do whatever it can to present our side of the story, because not everybody else will do that.

ELLIOTT: I would say, ideally, no, the government should not be involved in international broadcasting. But because there is no commercial potential for broadcasts from the United States in languages such as Bangla and Burmese, the government really does have to get involved if there's going to be any international broadcasting in those languages. Having said that, though, it would seem to me that if the major U.S. broadcasting news organizations, ABC, NBC, CBS, CNN, Fox, who make a lot of profit using public resources, could get together in a consortium, this is a way they could give back to the United States by providing an international broadcasting service at no cost to U.S. taxpayers. As a private entity, it would have that

---

William A. Rugh was a Foreign Service officer for thirty-one years.

Kim Andrew Elliott is an audience research analyst in the U.S. International Broadcasting Bureau. The views expressed here are his own, and not necessarily those of the IBB.

layer of independence that you just can't get if you are a government-funded organization. Furthermore, I don't think U.S. government broadcasting should compete with private efforts, as mentioned in the International Broadcasting Act of 1994. So, for that reason, it would be difficult to justify a global English television channel. They already exist.

HEIL: The content, however, is quite different in commercial broadcasting than it is in international broadcasting. Do you think this kind of consortium would serve the national interest and actually increase knowledge around the world in its broadest sense if there were no U.S. international broadcaster?

ELLIOTT: I think CNN International certainly provides education and information about the United States and about the world. It's a respectable international news organization. It's not everybody's cup of tea, but it's doing pretty much the same as what a U.S. government–funded international broadcasting service would do, so yes, I think it's possible.

HEIL: Now, some have suggested that U.S. international broadcasting has lost its way since the beginning of the twenty-first century. Do you agree or disagree, and if you agree, what two or three steps would you suggest that the next administration and the U.S. Congress take to fix it?

RUGH: I tend to agree. My focus and my interest have been broadcasting to the Middle East and North Africa, so I can speak to that domain. Specifically, I believe it has lost its way because broadcasting in Arabic to the Middle East has declined dramatically. The Voice of America Arabic Service on radio, I thought, did an excellent job. It had over the years built up an audience, built up a reputation, built up a style and an approach to the Middle East and North African audience that I thought was practically as good as it could be in terms of content. The technical ability to reach all audiences wasn't what I had hoped it could be, but that could be fixed as long as the content was good.

When the Broadcasting Board of Governors abolished Voice of America Arabic and created Radio Sawa, the concept may have been good, but in the implementation, it was a failure. And the creation of Alhurra television in Arabic, I think, has also failed, primarily because the content is poor. The reach of Radio Sawa, using FM primarily, isn't bad, but the content doesn't compare with quality of the content of VOA Arabic in my opinion, and in the opinion of nearly everybody I talk to in the region. By the same token, Alhurra Television has failed because of content, I think, in the sense that it's not appropriate, not relevant, not professional enough, and it is not interesting to the audience. It has failed in keeping its audience and providing what could be offered to an Arab audience. You ask what two or three steps could be taken. A simple step would be to go back to VOA Arabic, because they were doing it well, and doing it correctly. As for television, the content needs to be improved. There needs to be oversight by independent analysts who have the capability to judge the content in terms of the audience, in terms of the language, in terms of what is being provided by America to an Arab audience. And that requires several characteristics. If I were to design an oversight or review body, I would hire people who are bilingual—they wouldn't have to be native speakers, but that would be better—who have a deep understanding of professional journalism, and who know the Arab world, not just one or two countries but the whole region. That's been a failing of Alhurra. I would also hire people who know the United States very well. Now, every review board member doesn't have to have all those characteristics, but ideally, that would be the case. But those are essential to understand how to present the United States to the Arab world.

HEIL: Kim, as host of the VOA English program, *Communications World*, and as a scholar looking at all international broadcasting organizations in addition to those of the United States, what steps would you take—beyond the Middle East and in the rest of the world—what steps would you take to fix U.S. international broadcasting, assuming you feel that it needs to be fixed?

ELLIOTT: U.S. international broadcasting has always been a little bit off track, in that has tended to emphasize the needs of the U.S. government rather than the needs of the audience. One other sign that it has even further lost its way is that it continually subdivides itself into more and more entities that overlap and compete with each other. We're up to about six or seven such entities in U.S. international broadcasting. And in future conflicts, I would not be surprised if Congress creates new Radio Free radio stations that would duplicate what VOA is already doing in that same language. So as far as the two big steps are concerned: one would be rationalizing U.S. international broadcasting by combining the entities, and the second is to ensure the independence of U.S. international broadcasting so that it can achieve the credibility it needs to guarantee success. I think I'll be coming back to those two themes quite a bit today.

HEIL: One of the points that many have made is that it is necessary to have certain floor levels, or benchmarks, for broadcasting. For example, broadcasting in the U.N. languages would make some sense for U.S.–funded broadcasting as well as some of the small languages mentioned earlier.

> U.S. international broadcasting has always been a little bit off track, in that has tended to emphasize the needs of the U.S. government rather than the needs of the audience. One other sign that it has even further lost its way is that it continually subdivides itself into more and more entities that overlap and compete with each other.
>
> —Elliott

What would you say would be some minimum benchmarks for U.S. broadcasting, in terms of languages as well as the technical reach of the radio, TV, and Internet services?

ELLIOTT: I would not set any minimums. I would rather go with what the market will bear. You just need to go out and look at the countries that have a need for information because they're not getting it domestically from their state-controlled media, and you look at the language communities who need information, and then you decide, well, is this language or this country important enough for the U.S. government to broadcast in—or are there enough people speaking the language? I think there's a tendency now to go with just the larger countries and ignore the smaller countries. You remember from the invasion of Panama and the invasion of Grenada that smaller countries are sovereign enough to create mischief. They can harbor terrorists, they can abuse human rights, they can provide bases for enemies. Just because a country is small, it should not be ignored. Those are the benchmarks that I would set.

HEIL: Bill, I know that you, having served for many years in the Middle East, were able not only to follow very closely the VOA Arabic Service, but also the English service, and there have been moves lately to steadily diminish worldwide English on the Voice of America, which is the only U.S. government–funded international broadcaster that broadcasts in English. What's your take on that? Should English be one of the fundamental benchmarks?

RUGH: Absolutely. I think, focusing on North Africa and the Middle East, we've got to broadcast in English. English is widely spoken in the Arab world. There are a lot more people who speak English in the Arab world than there are Americans who speak Arabic, and to some extent, it's a one-way discussion in commercial media. We need to participate with those audiences who prefer to listen in English. There are many educated Arabs who have a fluency in English, in spoken English, and they'd probably rather listen in many cases to the original. If it's a president, or the secretary of state, or a congressman, or a commentary by a prominent American, many Arabs would rather hear it English than try to figure out what the original English was by listening to the Arabic. For benchmarks, to answer your question, English, Arabic, and French are absolutely essential, and we can't give up English. Also, because others—

> Focusing on North Africa and the Middle East, we've got to broadcast in English. Also, because others—the competition—are broadcasting in English, it would be ridiculous for the United States to give up broadcasting in our native language.
> —Rugh

the competition—are broadcasting in English, it would be ridiculous for the United States to give up broadcasting in our native language. Another benchmark is that on radio, we should focus on medium wave and FM.

I've always believed that shortwave is not very useful in the Arab world; it may be useful in other parts of the world, but we put a lot of money into shortwave transmitters that are not useful for Arab audiences. So I would put our money into FM and medium wave agreements to the extent that we can.

HEIL: As you've mentioned, shortwave is less important, but it can become very important in a crisis. But it is a new world, and it is a world of digital distribution. It's world in which Internet users are producing their own news and informational programming. Who do we need most to reach? We can't do everything. We've got to make hard choices. Who do we need most to reach in this digital age?

ELLIOTT: Well, you mentioned all these sources of news on the Internet. That's a lot of blogs. Blogging is an interesting phenomenon, but I don't think it's a primary news source for serious consumers of news. People still are going to turn to serious news sources, whether they're newspapers, news agencies, broadcasting organizations like BBC, CNN, and they'll consume the news from their original media and from Web sites and other Internet-delivered media. If U.S. international broadcasting is going to be a part of that, it's going to have to be perceived as a serious news organization on a par with some of those others, like the New York Times, CNN, and the BBC. The only way it can do that is to combine all those six or seven newsrooms into one formidable newsroom so it can have a world class news operation that people will actually turn to. Then you also have to ensure that this news organization has the independence it needs to be a credible organization. Otherwise, people aren't going to go to it. The audience for that kind of content—news and information—tends to be elite. That's the natural audience for international broadcasting.

There are a few exceptional circumstances where U.S. international broadcasting can reach mass audiences through entertainment, such as providing popular music to Iran, music absolutely absent from Iranian media. When those few exceptional situations are available, we should exploit them, but this is not going to happen very often.

HEIL: Do you think, Bill, looking at this from a distance, that we're agile enough to make the changes that are required in this post-Cold War, post-9/11 media environment?

RUGH: We should be. We've got the technical capabilities. We could spend the money on expanding them, on expanding the personnel and the hours of broadcast. There's no reason we can't compete, and it bothers me that we're not competing effectively. The new broadcasting services going to the Middle East have failed. They shouldn't have. There were high expectations when they began. Arab audiences said, "Oh this is going to be wonderful; we'll have American television in Arabic." And when they turned it on, they realized that it wasn't worth watching. And that's sad; that hurts our reputation.

If we're going to be in the game at all, we need to do it, and do it right. I agree with Kim about the problem of fragmentation. I think he's absolutely right. We need much more coordination. And there's another aspect to it. You have different agencies of the U.S. government pulling in different directions. We've got the State Department with a residual involvement in broadcasting, much smaller than it used to be. We've got the Pentagon doing a lot of broadcasting in many fields; they're doing Web sites, they're doing a lot of press work and media work, not only in Iraq, which started it, but in many places. It doesn't seem to me to be well coordinated at all.

I may have a slightly different take than Kim on the question of independence and the private sector because I believe that the Voice of America, in its heyday, before the BBG changed things at the end of the last decade, had found a formula that combined independence and journalism of integrity, on the one hand, with a fair presentation of American policy. I know that there were some who thought there was too much policy, or too much State Department involvement in the broadcasting. I think it was always worked out fairly well. There were occasional differences. But

I look back with nostalgia on the days that the Voice of America had that credibility all over the world, and especially in the Middle East. It was able to include credible news reporting with a responsible presentation of U.S. policy. In comparison, I've watched Alhurra television in the Middle East, and I've watched Al Jazeera. Al Jazeera, in my opinion, does a much better job of presenting American policy and American stories than Alhurra does. That's ridiculous.

HEIL: Kim, speaking of cost effectiveness, is U.S. international broadcasting at the present level, getting its money's worth in terms of appropriated funds?

ELLIOTT: I would say no, and the main evidence for that is that the U.S. spends more for international broadcasting than Britain does, but BBC has a larger audience than all of U.S. international broadcasting combined. The BBC global broadcasting budget is right around $500 million; for U.S. broadcasting, it's about $670 million. Now, you do have to correct for apples and oranges, but I think when you do, the contrast is even greater. The global audience for all of U.S. international broadcasting apparently is around 150 to 155 million, whereas for the BBC services—all the media put together—it's 233 million. If you take just VOA, it's 115 million weekly; for the BBC, it's 183 million. Just take one example, Burma. The BBC reaches 20 percent of the Burmese adults weekly, probably more during the present crisis, whereas VOA plus Radio Free Asia unduplicated reaches 17 million less than the BBC. So this U.S. system of transmitting to a country with two stations, where you have to tune into one station to get half the news, and to the other station to get the other half of the news, does not add value; it subtracts value. That's one of the reasons why I continue to advocate a rationalization of U.S. international broadcasting.

HEIL: There is the argument that new technologies in international broadcasting require additional resources, and that in order to meet those demands and expand priority services, cuts in core programs are necessary. Does that not suggest a need for additional funding, given all the new demands?

ELLIOTT: Well, we should keep the budget stable, the budget we have now, and then if you can catch up with the BBC, which has a greater audience and smaller budget, you can think about increasing the budget. Until there's some cost effectiveness in the way U.S. international broadcasting is organized, then I don't think increases in the budget would be warranted.

RUGH: I would take that last caveat to say that we should do both: increase the quality of the programming and increase the budget. I think we ought to be able to increase the quality and I would not use the excuse of poor quality to say the budget is enough. I guess that's not really what you said, but in the context of the money we are spending on the military and other international programs, we should certainly spend more money on broadcasting, but on the condition that we spend it properly in a coordinated fashion, focusing on quality and thinking about reaching the audience rather than just putting out what we think is best.

ELLIOTT: I'd just like to add briefly, though, that there are a lot of opportunities for savings; transmitting via the Internet is a lot cheaper than transmitting shortwave, so there may be opportunities for actually decreasing budget even though we're getting into new media. Now television is another animal altogether; that absolutely requires an increase in the budget.

HEIL: What about programming quality in all this? How do you generate the will to produce programming of the highest quality on all of the networks? Do you do it evenly, do you allow each of them to set their own programming agendas? Do they share information, as you said, by supplying a single newsroom? How do you do it?

ELLIOTT: The audience really tells you what they want. If you ask in group surveys what media they use and what topics they want covered, they report that they want quality information; they want the kind of information that benefits the United States to report because it sets the record straight and makes sure that people are not under any illusion about what U.S. actions and policies are overseas. And that's all helped along by the competition provided by the BBC and by other international broadcasters such as Radio Australia and Radio France Internationale. If we get serious about competing with the regional broadcasters, I think that will help you achieve the quality you are looking for.

RUGH: In the Arab world, the competition has grown intense over the last decade with the advent of satellite television in Arabic. There are now more than 370 TV channels in Arabic. Radio is still listened to, but competition is intense. The Internet is a competitive factor, but the audience for the Internet is still pretty small. It's going to grow, so it's important. I would say we should think more about presenting, as Kim says, what the audience wants, and if I can judge correctly, it wants to know more about the United States. We're trying too hard to compete with Al Jazeera on its own terms, and we can't do that. We can present news about Iraq, about Palestine and Israel and about all the crises that occur, and we should do that. But we'll never be able to match, in terms of reporting on events in the region, the reach, the intensity, and the speed of Al Jazeera, Al Arabiya, and the other Arab broadcasters. So I would say: continue to do that, but do a lot more reporting on the United States. We should do as much as we can to report daily life in America, American society, American culture, and American politics, and to give the Arab listener in his or her own terms—that's why it requires somebody sensitive to both cultures—to give that listener a clearer understanding than he or she has had of the United States; that ought to be possible.

There have been broadcasters in the past like Alistair Cooke who have given brilliant BBC reports on America to European audiences. That kind of program is lacking on international broadcasting sponsored by the United States today. There are people who could do it. I know Arab Americans who could be hired today and who could do that kind of thing. So in terms of quality, starting with Kim's recommendation that we offer what the audience wants, give them more about America. And I don't think that just because we're funded by the U.S. government, that turns people off. They'll listen to us anyway. Arabs are used to listening to and watching government-sponsored channels. They know how to discount it, they know how to take it with a grain of salt. We shouldn't worry about that. We should just go ahead and broadcast as best we can an honest portrayal of America.

ELLIOTT: If I might add to that, I think there is a finite appetite for news and information about the United States in the Arab world and in pretty much every target country. However, in the Arab world, that could be a pretty interesting niche for Alhurra, a U.S. Arabic language television channel, especially when the BBC Arabic channel comes on line and clobbers us in providing target country news and world news.

And what Ambassador Rugh says about knowing both cultures, the capability of being an intercultural communicator: that's the magic key right there. If you can find that talent—it's very hard to find—and they could be a window on America, somehow translating those two cultures, you could be onto something. It would be a station with enough of an audience to make it worthwhile.

HEIL: What about the role of nongovernment organizations and nonprofit producers, particularly television? These are rapidly expanding: one thinks of Sesame Street, Search for Common Ground, Layalina TV in the Middle

East. How do they fit into an overall future media strategy for public diplomacy?

ELLIOTT: I think the government should not try to coordinate any aspect of broadcasting or the media as far as content is concerned. Now it could make a public-private partnership just from an administrative angle. That would be okay, but it has got to stay out of the content.

RUGH: I agree. The government shouldn't even think about trying to control or coordinate the private sector, but there are many private-sector products that U.S.–sponsored international broadcasting can use, and it would be wasteful not to be open-minded about trying to use some of the wonderful programs that have been produced by the private sector for television, radio, and other media. It's something that we should be glad about, to an extent, unless it gives a false picture and distorts. But in the Arab world, certainly the wealthy countries have bought a lot of programs from the United States on their own. They haven't waited for the U.S. government to do them, and they haven't tried to duplicate them on their own. So there's a lot of American commercial material on Arab television already, without us even trying, and a lot of it is useful.

HEIL: Well, in connection with U.S. government–sponsored overseas programming, it's said by some that interactivity will be to international broadcasting in the twenty-first century what shortwave was in the twentieth century in the sense that the more opportunities there are for dialogue and call-ins, the more useful the broadcasts will be for audiences. What formats would you suggest to shape such a dialogue?

RUGH: I'm a big fan of interactivity. In the 1980s and 1990s, when VOA was doing interactive call-in shows, I thought they were the best programs we were doing. That was particularly the case for policymakers sitting in America who are used to answering questions from Americans. So the answers they give, the speeches they make that are unilateral, are often off the subject and don't deal with the questions that are on the minds of the audience. I saw many wonderful, successful call-in shows on VOA in Arabic or in English, in which policymakers sitting in Washington would be forced to fashion a response to a question that he or she usually didn't get from domestic audiences because that's what was on the mind of the questioner. They're terrific, and they've expanded in the Arab world in their own media. Television and radio within the Arab region has made much more use of call-in shows. So it's something that is popular, and it's very effective.

HEIL: Looking beyond the Arab world, Kim, which areas of the globe today are ripest for interactive programming?

ELLIOTT: The best international broadcasting all along was interactive, way back before the Internet. Probably one of the most halfway decent programs on Radio Moscow, which had very few decent programs, was *Moscow Mailbag* with Joe Adamov. He answered questions and he provided short, interesting answers. Even though it was propaganda, it was interesting. And then there was Jonathan Marks and his *Media Network* program on Radio Netherlands to a large extent written by the audience. People in the audience would send in snippets of audio, and it would become a large part of the show. And that's why I stole his format for my program, *Communications World*, on the Voice of America. I received cassette tapes, letters, and all of that became part of the news package that was part of my show. We became a community of people who would tune in every week to hear what the rest of the community was saying. Then, the Internet came along and made it all better, made it easier, quicker to get the information from the audience. Audio could be sent via the Internet rather than through the mail, so it was all sped up quite a bit. So the Internet just facilitates a good part of international broadcasting. On VOA, the *Talk to America* show was getting a little tired toward the end of its run. The same few people were calling in, over and over. Many of their questions did not pertain. But the Internet made it possible for VOA to do a format change in a show like that, so that the questions that came via email or voice mail could be edited down into interesting bits. VOA could have the show less often: once a week instead of every day. You do have to adapt interactive formats over time.

HEIL: Looking ahead, say ten years, what is your vision for U.S. international broadcasting? What potentially might inspire policymakers and Congress about the value of this profession?

RUGH: Well, I don't have a crystal ball, but ten years from now, it is certainly likely that the Internet will be much, much bigger than it is today in the Arab world and around the world. It's limited still today, but it's a growth industry. There are some efforts by the State Department and in the Pentagon, certainly, to get involved in the Internet, but I believe we ought to think about it much more deeply and develop capabilities because it's not as easily controlled as unilateral broadcasting. It's interactive. It can be anonymous, and it's a medium that's instantaneous, so you have to be quick on your feet to be able to keep up with the discussion and the dialogue. Those are challenges that I think we're capable of meeting. As far as radio and television are concerned, I think that radio will still be a useful medium ten years from now. It may take different forms; I think medium wave will still be useful, shortwave will still be useful. Television is less certain, because it has grown so fast, at least in the area that I know about, that it's a little harder to predict where it's going to be a decade from now. The Arabic services that have been recently developed by the French, the Russians, and others—and now the BBC is going back to Arabic television—may or may not survive. I would guess that the BBC has a better chance of surviving because it already has a very solid reputation for the quality of its radio broadcasts. For years, it has developed a following, an audience that I think will help the BBC television people, and I presume they'll do as good a job as the radio people.

HEIL: Kim?

ELLIOTT: My vision would involve six points. I wrote about this around 1990 in my article in *Foreign Policy*, "Too Many Voices of America?" It's much the same now. First, I would privatize U.S. international broadcasting a much as possible; completely, if possible, but it's kind of far-fetched at this point. Second, rationalize U.S. international broadcasting by combining the entities into one formidable unit. Third, ensure the independence of U.S. international broadcasting so that it can have that credibility. Fourth, conduct public diplomacy as a separate activity, under a separate agency, in a separate building, preferably in a separate city. In many target countries, when they develop competent, fairly free journalism, the function for U.S. international broadcasting dissipates, disappears, but there's always public diplomacy because people need to know what the U.S. government position is. So public diplomacy will survive into perpetuity; international broadcasting in many target countries will expire. Fifth, select broadcast languages with at least as much attention to the audience needs as to the needs of the U.S. government. And sixth, decision makers should not forget that the primary function of U.S. international broadcasting is to get information into countries where that information is otherwise restricted. Therefore you have to use the media that can get through. That's not always the sexiest medium. It may not be television, it may not be the Internet. You may have to rely on good old-fashioned shortwave because it is still the least interdictable of the mass media available to international broadcasting.

RUGH: May I comment? I agree with all of that except for the separation of public diplomacy. My concept of public diplomacy and international broadcasting is that they work together and that international broadcasting as carried out by the Voice of America in the past was an essential part of public diplomacy. Public diplomacy is not just policy advocacy; it's much, much more than policy advocacy. It is Americana, explaining America, and portraying America, including dissent and disagreement. And so I wouldn't confine public diplomacy to an official U.S. government spokesman announcing and explaining policy. That's only a part of it. For the needs of public diplomacy in my concept, we really need a credible international broadcasting system to include all the media that we've been talking about and in the languages that are useful, not just in denied countries, but in countries where we need to be a part of the dialogue in a rapidly changing world.

Conclusions and Recommendations

Alan L. Heil Jr.

A RENAISSANCE in international broadcasting's mission and strategic goals
is essential to regaining the respect the United States enjoyed worldwide
throughout much of the twentieth century. The time is ripe. America's
newest generation, as Tom Brokaw recently put it, is poised "on the frontier
of an empowering era."[1]

U.S. international broadcasting that empowers those seeking freedom
and justice is also a pressing national security need. An arc of crises encompasses
Burma, Tibet, Pakistan, Iran, Iraq, Israel, Palestine, Lebanon, Georgia, and
Russia. Unstable environments enable the growth of terrorism, and nuclear
proliferation among state and non-state actors is another clear threat. In a
volatile world, sudden crises could require equally sudden and unanticipated
U.S. military interventions, even as new policies of collaboration and
dialogue are emerging. Unfortunately, in these tumultuous times, America's
reputation abroad is at an all-time low among both adversaries and allies. It
continues to decline, imperiling the nation's safety and eroding its economic
and political clout. With the advent of a new administration and new
Congress, the time to confront this slide is now.

International broadcasting is an essential component of U.S. security
and influence. Accurate and objective real-time information is important
for people everywhere and crucial to those in areas of conflict. In addition,
through specific programming and by example, U.S. broadcasting overseas
can reflect our nation's best values. Today, publicly funded civilian
broadcasting overseas promotes U.S. security and integrity for about one
tenth of one percent of what is spent on national defense. As Secretary
of Defense Robert M. Gates recently said, "This country must strengthen
other important elements of national power both institutionally and
financially, and create the capability to integrate and apply all the elements
of national power to problems and challenges abroad." Quoting Chairman
Lantos of the House Foreign Affairs Committee, Secretary Gates asked,
"'How has one man in a cave managed to out-communicate the world's
greatest communications society?' Speed, agility, and cultural relevance

are not terms that come readily to mind when discussing U.S. strategic communications."[2]

Grounded on the data, experience, and informed views of this book's contributors, the Public Diplomacy Council urges Congress and the administration to conduct an in-depth examination of the each of the five principal networks (VOA, RFE/RL, RFA, the Martis, and the MBN) and of the coordination among them. This survey should explore for the first time the programming and online or video capabilities of the nongovernmental, nonprofit public service broadcasters, whose growth has been virtually unnoticed. How do the efforts of nongovernmental broadcasters relate to and potentially enhance the messages offered by the U.S.–funded networks? The current administration and the Congress have increased broadcasting outlays since 9/11, but are the increases sufficient? Have they occurred in the most cost-effective broadcasting networks? Do they meet global needs, as well as those in priority regions? The urgently needed survey of our all of our overseas broadcasts—government-funded and private nonprofit—must be followed by specific policy recommendations.

At a conference on U.S. international broadcasting in Cantigny Park, Illinois, in April 2007, former Federal Communications Commission Chairman Newton Minow lamented what he called the "whisper" of America. He said,

> Although the Voice of America, and later other international radio services, have made valuable contributions, they suffer today from miserly funding. In many areas of the world, they have been seldom more than a whisper. People in every country know our music, our movies, our clothes, and our sports. But they do not know our freedom or our values or our democracy.

Minow reiterated his suggestion of five years earlier that America invest the equivalent annually of 1 percent of the U.S. defense budget in public diplomacy, which would more than triple the current public diplomacy expenditure. More than $5 billion for U.S. overseas information and cultural programs in 2009 would be "one dollar to launch ideas," as Minow put it, "for every $100 we invest to launch bombs."

A Public Diplomacy Council consensus endorses streamlining the structure of international broadcasting and acquiring the necessary resources to fulfill these principal goals:

1. Restore VOA radio services and core languages such as worldwide English and Russian to pre-2001 levels, and restore

as much of the transmission structure as possible. Nearly half of U.S. international broadcasting AM and shortwave transmitters have been shut down or abolished in the past five years.

2. Reconstitute the BBG as a bipartisan, independent governmental body exercising broad oversight and reporting to both the Congress and the Executive branch. Members should collectively possess expertise in media, international affairs (including public diplomacy), journalism, business, and education. Vacancies on the Board and expired terms should be filled quickly.

3. Reduce the support staff of the new board or agency to allow the heads of the component broadcast networks to conduct day-to-day management, and hold them accountable for the quality and strategic impact of the services in today's rapidly evolving communications environment.

4. Redirect the mission to reflect a U.S. emphasis on collaboration— rather than confrontation—in its foreign relations; for example, co-produce more programs with community stations abroad.

5. Strengthen monitoring of the broadcasts and content research to track new broadcasting technologies and to identify, region by region, the best mixes of media in a growing viral media environment.

6. Establish minimum long-range, strategic benchmarks for preserving core programming: central news and operations and radio services in English and other United Nations languages, as well as languages in regions judged imperative to the national interest, including those in countries beyond the Muslim world where media are restricted or censored.

7. Ensure that communication of news, analysis, and factual information is aimed at those of influence in governmental, business, academic, scientific, and opinion shaping communities overseas. Make a liberal but subsidiary use of other content such as feature material, music, and entertainment. Programming quality rather than audience size is paramount.

8. Recommend that Congress rescind section 501 of the Smith-Mundt Act (HR 3342) of 1947 to permit distribution in the United States of materials prepared for dissemination abroad by U.S.–funded civilian agencies, including international broadcast content.

Public Diplomacy Council President Robert T. Coonrod and other contributors to this book envision an even broader scope for those studying future horizons for U.S. international broadcasting. While the reconstituted Broadcasting Board of Governors that assumed charge in June 2007 has signaled an interest in a fresh start in 2009, there must be better coordination by the BBG or its successors with the growing number of nongovernmental public service program producers such as Search for Common Ground, Sesame Workshop, Layalina TV, ITVS International, and America Abroad. A necessarily loose coordination of programming among all government and nongovernmental multimedia would augur well for enhanced cost effectiveness and increased resources for much of U.S. international broadcasting, public and private.

Our electronic dialogue with others around the world must be expanded and enriched. It must be an inherent part of the stunning evolution in communications described in these pages. Our interlocutors must include those of high station in the world's political and commercial capitals, as well as those millions who are barely surviving in nearby slums or in vast rural reaches of the planet. We must reach the same audiences that terrorists endeavor to reach; we must confront insurgents in their own blogosphere. A multimedia dialogue must begin with and be sustained by greatly enhanced U.S. listening skills, whether on audio, video, or Internet channels.

Listening to and assessing one's audience is a precondition for sound program design. In a landmark study in 2007, two research specialists of RFE/RL, Daniel Kimmage and Kathleen Ridolfo, examined online insurgent media in Iraq over a period of several months. Based on analysis of the insurgents' blogs, press releases, and advanced video production techniques using cell phone cameras, they arrived at a sobering conclusion: all were designed to recruit terrorists throughout the Arab world in real time. But Kimmage and Ridolfo concluded that the terrorist propagandists' apparent strengths—decentralization and flexibility—were also their greatest weaknesses. Their findings had an impact on RFE/RL programming, and were widely distributed throughout the U.S. government.[3]

Most important, new U.S. international broadcasting must have an impact on daily conversations in distant lands. A solid foundation already exists. For example:

> President of Albania Alfred Moisiu said on a recent trip to Washington that the Voice of America's Albanian Service was his daily companion in not just one, but two media. Moisiu, leader of a Muslim majority country, said that he listens on his Walkman to the news on VOA every morning as he walks around his neighborhood. At work, he often shares what he

has heard with his cabinet, and at times, he asks ministries to act on issues raised during VOA news programs. Then, when wrapping up his day at the office, he turns on his television to catch VOA Albanian (also widely viewed in neighboring Kosovo, which remains a potential flashpoint eight years after the NATO intervention.) President Moisiu presented the VOA with an Albanian medal of freedom in 2006 to thank the Albanian Service for its work.[4]

A 38-year-old Burmese laborer recently wrote Radio Free Asia to thank the network for its educational programming. "Even though I am not an educated person, RFA's programs have enabled me to talk like one," he said. "A few months ago, I explained the Universal Declaration of Human Rights to a son of the businessman I work for. When I finished the explanation, the son and his mother asked me how I learned about it because they were in disbelief that a coolie with only a middle school education could have a sophisticated understanding of world politics. I explained that I had learned it from foreign radio broadcasts, and that I listened regularly to RFA and the BBC."[5]

In ways that are unique in public diplomacy, broadcasting—publicly or privately funded—can reach millions of people either in real time or in documentaries that foster dialogue, collaboration, and conflict resolution now and in future generations. Under these circumstances, the United States simply cannot afford to reduce the quality or reach of its government-funded international broadcast networks, nor can it undermine the credibility or brands that have earned those networks loyal overseas audiences over the years. Rather, it must summon the will to strengthen its only instantaneous means of reaching millions who look to America as a beacon of hope as they once did in a bipolar world. These sturdy pillars and sufficient resources are fundamental as the nation builds a new U.S. international broadcasting approach attuned to the era of both promise and peril that lies ahead.

Notes

1.   Tom Brokaw, commencement address, Santa Fe College, New Mexico, May 15, 1999.
2.   Robert M. Gates, Landon Lecture, Kansas State University, Nov. 26, 2007.

3.   "Iraq: RFE/RL Report Reveals Extent of Sunni-Insurgent Media Network," RFE/RL news release, June 24, 2007.

4.   VOA Eurasia Division Director Elez Biberaj, email, December 17, 2007.

5.   RFA Director of Congressional Liaison John Estrella, email, Dec. 12, 2007.

Appendix 1. International Broadcasting Act, 1994

The International Broadcasting Act of 1994 (Public Law 103-236) states that all United States publicly funded international broadcasting under the jurisdiction of the U.S. Broadcasting Board of Governors shall:

- Be conducted in accordance with the highest professional standards of broadcast journalism.
- Be based on reliable information about its potential audience.
- Be designed so as to effectively reach a significant audience.
- Promote respect for human rights, including freedom of religion.
- Produce programming to meet the needs that remain unserved by the totality of media voices available to the people of certain nations.
- Offer information about developments in each significant region of the world.
- Present a variety of opinions and voices from within particular nations and regions prevented by censorship or repression from speaking to their fellow countrymen.

APPENDIX 2.   VOICE OF AMERICA

VOA is the nation's largest publicly funded, global civilian multimedia network among the five entities administered by the BBG. It operates under a charter approved by Congress as Public Laws 94-350 and 103-415:

"The long-range interests of the United States are served by communicating directly with the people of the world by radio. To be effective, the Voice of America must win the attention and respect of listeners. These principles will therefore govern Voice of America (VOA) broadcasts:

1. VOA will serve as a consistently reliable and authoritative source of news. VOA news will be accurate, objective and comprehensive.
2. VOA will represent America, not any single segment of American society, and will therefore present a balanced and comprehensive projection of significant American thought and institutions.
3. VOA will present the policies of the United States clearly and effectively, and will also present responsible discussion and opinion on these policies."

Signed by Presidents Gerald R. Ford (July 12, 1976) and Bill Clinton (October 24, 1994).

Appendix 3. Radio Free Europe/Radio Liberty

The mission of Radio Free Europe/Radio Liberty is to promote democratic values and institutions by disseminating factual information and ideas.

From Central Europe to the Pacific, from the Baltic to the Black Sea, from Russia to Central Asia to the Persian Gulf, countries are struggling to overcome autocratic institutions, violations of human rights, centralized economies, ethnic and religious hostilities, regional conflicts, and controlled media.

Stability—based on democracy and free-market economies—throughout this region is essential to global peace. Based on the conviction that the first requirement of democracy is a well informed citizenry, and building on nearly a half century of surrogate broadcasting to this region:

1. RFE/RL provides objective news, analysis, and discussion of domestic and regional issues crucial to successful democratic and free-market transformations.
2. RFE/RL strengthens civil societies by projecting democratic values.
3. RFE/RL combats ethnic and religious intolerance and promotes mutual understanding among peoples.
4. RFE/RL provides a model for local media, assists in training to enhance media professionalism and independence, and develops partnerships with local media outlets.
5. RFE/RL fosters closer ties between the countries of the region and the world's established democracies.

APPENDIX 4. RADIO FREE ASIA

Radio Free Asia adheres to the highest standards of journalism and strives for accuracy, balance and fairness in its editorial content. In addition to its news programming and commentaries, RFA broadcasts works of literature and nonfiction that have been banned in RFA's target countries.

RFA's mission is to provide accurate and timely information, news and commentary about events in Asia. It is a forum for a variety of opinions and voices from within Asian nations whose people do not fully enjoy freedom of expression.

As a surrogate broadcaster, RFA provides news and commentary specific to each of its target countries, acting as the free press these countries lack.

From RFA's Code of Ethics:

- We must maintain a calm, dispassionate tone and avoid polemics directed against any persons, groups or governments. We will not preach to or talk down to our listeners.
- We must not incite listeners to violence or encourage acts of rebellion or emigration. We provide a forum for a variety of ideas and opinions.
- Both online editors and broadcasters must ensure that no story that airs or that is published on the Web site is based on rumor or unsubstantiated information. Whenever possible, we must seek more than one source for a story.
- We must remain independent of any political party, opposition group, exile organization, or religious body and we shall not advocate any political viewpoint.
- We must clearly identify outside contributors, stating at the end of their commentaries that the opinions they express are not necessarily those of RFA.

APPENDIX 5. MIDDLE EAST BROADCASTING NETWORKS INC. (ALHURRA TELEVISION AND RADIO SAWA)

ALHURRA

Alhurra (Arabic for "The Free One") is a 24-hour Arabic language television channel operated by the Middle East Broadcasting Networks, Inc. Broadcast from studios near Washington, D.C., and bureaus throughout the Middle East, Alhurra is primarily news and information programming. In addition to reporting news of regional and international events, the channel provides information on a variety of subjects, including health and personal fitness, entertainment news, sports, fashion, and science and technology. It features talk shows, current affairs magazines, roundtable discussions, and debates. The station offers accurate, balanced, and comprehensive news and information programming utilizing the latest digital television technology and highest quality production values. The channel's news and information content endeavors to broaden the viewers' perspectives, enabling them to think for themselves and make better decisions.

   Mission: To broadcast accurate, timely, and relevant news and information about the region, the world, and the United States to a broad, Arabic speaking audience, and thereby, to advance freedom and democracy in the Middle East and long-term U.S. national interests.
Radio Sawa:

RADIO SAWA

Radio Sawa, a 24-hour, seven-days-a-week Arabic language network, is unique in the Middle East. It broadcasts objective, balanced, up-to-the-minute news and news analysis combined with an upbeat mix of the best Western and Arabic pop music. The station also broadcasts interviews, opinion pieces, sports and features on a wide variety of political and social issues.

   Mission: Radio Sawa seeks to effectively communicate with the youthful population of Arabic-speakers in the Middle East by providing up-to-date news, information and entertainment on the 24/7 FM and medium wave stations throughout the region. Its secondary target audience is news-seekers of all ages. Radio Sawa is committed to broadcasting accurate, timely, and relevant news about the Middle East, the world, and the United States, and thereby, advancing the long-term U.S. national interest of promoting freedom and democracy. Radio Sawa is committed to the highest standards of journalism, the free marketplace of ideas, respect for the intelligence and culture of its audience, and a style that is upbeat, modern, and forward looking.

APPENDIX 6. OFFICE OF CUBA BROADCASTING (RADIO AND TV MARTI)

The Office of Cuba Broadcasting directs the operations of Radio and TV Marti, which broadcast accurate and objective news and information on issues of interest to the people of Cuba. In accordance with the Broadcasting to Cuba Act of 1983 (Public Law 98-111), Radio Marti follows Voice of America journalistic standards and guidelines.

Radio Marti broadcasts news and a variety of features and news analysis around the clock on shortwave, AM, and the Internet (www.martinoticias.com.)

TV Marti produces eight hours of original programming daily, including two 30-minute newscasts. The station broadcasts commentary and information about events in Cuba and elsewhere to promote the free flow of information and ideas in that country.

GLOSSARY

AFP
Agence France Presse, the French News Agency.

AM
Amplitude modulation on radio, associated with the standard broadcast bands (550-1600 MHz on the radio dial in the United States). The term "AM" is often referred to by international broadcasters as medium wave.

Alhurra
A 24/7 U.S. government–funded, privately incorporated Arabic language television network located in Springfield, Virginia. See also MBN and Radio Sawa.

BBC
The British Broadcasting Corporation, encompassing both home and international services on radio, television, and the Internet. The World Service is on the air in thrity-three languages.

Broadcasting Board of Governors
The BBG is a federal agency that oversees all U.S. government–funded civilian overseas broadcasting networks (VOA, RFE/RL, Radio Free Asia, Radio and TV Marti and the Middle East Broadcast Network, MBN, consisting of Alhurra television and Radio Sawa).

BIB
The Board for International Broadcasting was the oversight body for Radio Free Europe/Radio Liberty until the U.S. Broadcasting Board of Governors assumed that role in 1995.

Blog
Short for Weblog. A Web site that contains written material, links, or photos, initiated by one individual or a group. Entries, called "posts," appear in chronological order and usually invite readers to comment. To blog: To run a blog or post material on one.

Circumventor
Software brand developed to help users in China and other countries whose governments attempt to block access to certain Internet sites.

Deutsche Welle
Germany's multimedia (radio, TV, and the Internet) international broadcasting arm, headquartered in Berlin and broadcasting in twenty-seven languages.

FM
Frequency modulation. FM uses a wider band than AM (shortwave and medium wave) producing higher fidelity for music programming.

G3 Media
Games on the Internet, a term derived from Global Games and Gaming.

Herzian Waves
Kilohertz designations on the radio broadcast spectrum.

IBB
The International Broadcasting Bureau is a federal civil service agency that provides many VOA and Radio and TV Marti support functions such as performance review, marketing, personnel, management services, and research. IBB also provides engineering and transmission for all U.S. government–funded civilian overseas networks.

IPod
A brand of portable media player introduced by Apple for which the first podcasting scripts were developed. *See also* Podcast.

IPTV
An acronym for Internet Protocol Television, a system in which digital television service is delivered using an Internet protocol over a network infrastructure.

MBN
The Middle East Broadcasting Networks is an umbrella organization overseeing the U.S. grantee Arabic language stations Alhurra television and Radio Sawa. These report through the MBN to the Broadcasting Board of Governors.

Mobile Platforms
New delivery means such a cell phone Web surfing, podcasts, mobile TV and a variety of other digital receivers.

MySpace

A global social networking Web site offering an interactive, user-submitted network of friends, personal profiles, blogs, groups, photos, music, and videos.

OCB

The Office of Cuba Broadcasting is an umbrella organization overseeing Radio and TV Marti Spanish language broadcasting to Cuba. The Miami-based network reports to the Broadcasting Board of Governors in Washington, D.C.

Peer-to-Peer Media Environment

Also known as P2P. Media streaming in large distributed systems such as the Internet, usually among collaborative users in industry, academia, and other fields with similar interests. A pure peer-to-peer network does not have the notion of clients or servers, but only equal peer nodes that simultaneously function as both "clients" and "servers" to the other nodes on the network. This model of network arrangement differs from the client-server model in which communication is usually to and from a central server.

Podcast

Contraction of "iPod" and "broadcasting." A digital file containing audio and/or video material, usually offered on a blog and sometimes by RSS feed, for audience members to download.

Post

Writing, image, or sound that is posted on a blog.

Radio Farda

An around-the-clock Persian language service to Iran administered by Radio Free Europe/Radio Liberty, headquartered in Prague, the Czech Republic.

Radio Sawa

The 24/7 Arabic language service headquartered in Springfield, Virginia, and overseen by the Middle East Broadcast Networks and the Broadcasting Board of Governors.

RCI

Radio Canada International, headquartered in Montreal, broadcasting in nine languages.

RFA

Radio Free Asia. This U.S.–funded grantee surrogate network is based in

Washington, D.C., and broadcasts in eight languages to information-denied areas of East and Southeast Asia.

RFE/RL

Radio Free Europe/Radio Liberty, a U.S.–funded grantee surrogate network, is located in Prague, the Czech Republic, and broadcasts in twenty-eight languages to the former Soviet Union, the Balkans, Central Asia, Iran, and Afghanistan.

RFI

Radio France Internationale is the official French overseas network, based in Paris and broadcasting in nineteen languages.

RSS

Really Simple Syndication. Allows a user to collect the latest items posted on a Web site. Especially suited for blogs because it alerts users whenever their favorite blogs are updated. It can also "syndicate" content by allowing other Web sites (simply and automatically to reproduce all or part of a site's content.

Second Life

A shared virtual environment accessible on a personal computer. Transports users to a variety of three-dimensional virtual worlds.

SMS

Short Message Services. A communications protocol allowing the interchange of short messages between mobile telephony devices. Also known as text messages.

Social Media

Media, usually online, that enable groups to communicate or collaborate. Examples include group authoring, as on blogs and wikis, and personal Web pages as in MySpace, Facebook, Flickr, or LinkedIn. See also Wikipedia.

USIA

United States Information Agency. From 1954 to 1999, this independent U.S. government agency reported directly to the president and administered the nation's overseas information and cultural programs, including VOA. USIA was consolidated into the Department of State on October 1, 1999.

Viral Media

The ability of Internet Web sites and peer-to-peer messaging systems to spread infective information that has impact across widely dispersed social networks and national borders.

Virus

A computer virus can copy itself and infect a computer when introduced through an email message or other source. The idea of spreading has led to terms like "viral marketing" and "viral video," where consumers are motivated to share messages, Web sites or other programs with their social networks.

VOA

Voice of America. The nation's only official and global international broadcast network, headquartered in Washington and broadcasting in forty-five languages. It is a federal agency, funded and chartered by Congress. Like the U.S.–funded grantees, its oversight organization is the Broadcasting Board of Governors.

Webcam

A portable personal computer that can take and transmit video anywhere in the world.

Web Chat

Web chats are online, text-based discussions that allow audiences to interact with a speaker through instant messaging. Technical settings may allow open attendance or limit access. The written nature of the event allows for a transcript if a participant captures the text and places it on a Web page.

Wiki

From the Hawaiian word "wikiwiki" (quick). A Web site that can be easily and quickly updated by any visitor. The word has also come to mean the tools used to create a wiki (wiki engines). Blogs and wikis have some similarities, but the wiki is used to allow many people to author a work together.

Wikipedia

An openly available online digital encyclopedia. Wikipedia permits editing and updating by any user in the system and is useful for many purposes. Offers an enormous and constantly evolving store of reference information.

INDEX